THE J

THE LIP

D0834142

QJW6

Equal Woman

Equal Woman:
A Christian Feminist
Perspective

MYRTLE LANGLEY

Marshalls

85 -00286 PTH
(AQJW6)

Marshalls Paperbacks
Marshall Morgan & Scott
3 Beggarwood Lane, Basingstoke, Hants, UK
Copyright © Myrtle Langley 1983
First published by Marshall Morgan & Scott 1983

All rights reserved. No part of this publication may be reproduced, stored
in a retrieval system, or transmitted, in any form or by any means,
electronic, mechanical, photocopying, recording or otherwise, without the
prior permission of the Copyright owner.

ISBN 0 551 01064 9

Printed and bound in Great Britain at
The Camelot Press Ltd, Southampton

JOHN RYLANDS
UNIVERSITY
LIBRARY

BIND

For Joyce

Contents

Foreword

Myrtle Langley has done me the honour of inviting me to contribute this Foreword to her latest book and I am glad to commend it for serious study. The author has already made a name for herself as writer, thinker and teacher, to which she has now added the attribute of missioner as well, and these are the qualifications which she has brought to her present work.

The book is directed primarily towards evangelical Christians and is a plea to those who share Dr. Langley's biblical presuppositions to re-examine their attitudes to the ministry and place of women in the light of the teaching of Scripture and the chequered experience of the Christian Church. It should not be surprising that occasionally a touch of passion shows through, for this is written not with the detachment of a sociological survey but the commitment of a believer grappling with issues of truth.

With a subject of such emotive intensity it would be unusual if this book did not arouse controversy and mixed reactions from its readers. But then the author does not want to be read simply by those who agree with her but by all who will take her evidence seriously. I like to think that is why she invited me to write this opening commendation. In any case, I should like to express my indebtedness to her for allowing me a first sight of her book in typescript and I hope that it will be read thoughtfully by many people and given the consideration which is its due.

JOHN ST. ALBANS

Preface

I begin this introductory study of Christian woman with a brief autobiographical sketch. For me, the raising of my 'woman consciousness' came late and continued throughout the period of researching and writing this book. To find one's perspective changing can be deeply painful as well as highly exhilarating. My experience overall, however, is that the discovery of a 'feminist' perspective has given me a new and fresh interpretation of history and a more resourceful and realistic approach to living. Nonetheless, it would be wrong to infer that I now see life only through feminist-coloured spectacles: this would be to ignore the equally valid and valuable views from other vantage points.

I tell my story very selectively in order to highlight issues which deeply affect women, Christian and non-Christian alike, and if women, then men, in today's world. And I argue with deep conviction rather than with academic detachment – although hopefully with cool logic and cumulative evidence as well – because I believe that a recognition of the fundamental equality between man and woman, as between Jew and Gentile, freeman and slave, is central to the gospel as lived by Jesus and preached by Paul.

I owe a debt of gratitude to those who have read and commented on various parts of my manuscript, although I have not always been able to incorporate their suggestions: John and Penny Applegate, Joyce Baldwin, Charmion Mann, John and Alice Parr, Christine Redgrave, and members of the Tyndale Fellowship Ethics Study Group. Special thanks are due to my editor, John Hunt, without whom there would have been no *Equal Woman*!

Diocese of Liverpool,   Myrtle S. Langley
November 1982

Part One:

INTRODUCTION

1: Journey to Nowhere
Woman in a man's world

I was born, the eldest of three children, in an Irish village, just one month after the beginning of World War II. Food was rationed and luxuries were hard to come by. But the father in my child's world was a businessman and somehow or other he managed to conjure up chocolate eggs at Eastertime and toys for our Christmas stockings. Some of my earliest and most vivid and exciting memories are associated with my mother creeping out to early communion on Christmas morning while I investigated and lovingly handled the new trainset, tractor or motorcar. I never played with dolls; well, not seriously: they were for my sister and her friends. Similarly all my early playmates were boys. With them I romped the fields and played at cowboys and indians, erecting wigwams and tree-top dwellings and fashioning bows and arrows. And when it came to films, in those halcyon days of the cinema, I accompanied my father to westerns and wondered how ever anyone could tolerate the sentimental 'trash' of forties and early fifties romance. Yes, by conventional wisdom and in family opinion, I was both a 'tomboy' and a 'daddy's girl'.

Yet a girl I was, and I never recall aspiring to any other than what was clearly recognised as a woman's career – that is, unless frequently playing the officiating clergyman indicated an unconscious vocation! Three professions only were open to women in my village world: teaching, nursing and being a secretary. The last mentioned I rejected because it appeared to involve too much time at the desk and not enough with people; nursing I shied away from because of the bloodiness of it all (not that I am in any way squeamish); and so, teaching remained. I had often enough heard my parents express the opinion that I would never marry and at that time in Ireland primary teaching (the only kind I knew) was

15

the preserve of the 'spinster' or 'old maid'. Moreover, she was as much an institution in village life as the clergyman and the doctor, very much a professional person in her own right. It was only later, through the influence of the ubiquitous missionary lantern lecture held in the schoolhouse during the long winter evenings and the missionary biography – Mary Slessor of Calabar I recall – that I vowed to be a missionary teacher. Religion was an integral part of life: all life crises from the cradle to the grave were blessed by the church and there was virtually no social life without it. To believe in God was only natural and reasonable, so that to follow him 'into the church' or 'onto the mission field' was understandable if not always desirable.

Village life, as I grew up to know it, properly belonged to the pre-industrial age. Certainly, there were rich and poor – landed gentry and labouring tenants and workers. But the vast majority made up a society of farmers and shopkeepers, publicans and artisans. And everybody knew the clergy, the doctor, the teacher, the banker, the midwife and the police. There was no industrial working class and few if any upper-middle or upper-class genteel ladies of the kind familiar to the Victorian age. There was little alienation: life seemed to be woven whole. I saw no exploitation of the working woman, except in the home where she bore and cared for a large brood of children (I knew one who had borne twenty-one, of whom seventeen had survived), and was often brutally beaten by her husband. But I grew up with little awareness of the idea that women were somehow inferior to men. Admittedly they were different but they frequently performed similar if not identical tasks. True, wives stayed at home to look after the children and men did not encroach in the areas of childcare or domestic chores. But women as well as men made the hay, milked the cows, drove the tractor, fed the farm animals, served behind the bar and drove the taxis. The modern suburban housewife was unknown. Women had their menfolk near at hand and, normally, grandparents, aunties and uncles, brothers and sisters and numerous cousins provided the companionable and useful world of the extended family. So, although a woman's place may have been in the home, that home was no ivory castle but an integral part of a workaday world. However, one common 'patriarchal saying', indicative of male dominance, I did pick up quite clearly; it was this: a woman must not dare to 'wear the trousers'.

Thus it was that as I left the village primary school to embark on the second stage of my life which would take me in turn to a local convent, boarding school, college and university I had little if any consciousness of sexism. And several years spent in residential female institutions in no way changed the situation. My father had great ambitions for me and so long as I remained at the top academically he was satisfied. And when competitiveness featured it was between people, as we all belonged to the same sex. Male teachers didn't upset the pattern.

While in my first year at boarding school I underwent on evangelical conversion. As a result I set my sights ever more strongly on the mission field, throwing myself into the work of the Christian Union and helping to run mission-oriented girls' camps and Inter-varsity evangelistic campaigns. And there seemed to be no limit to the work I could undertake as a woman. For me, woman in the church meant woman in the church overseas where women outnumbered men by two to one.

After qualifying as a primary schoolteacher I took a job in a midlands town, moving later to be near the city so that I could finish my degree and take a diploma in education. I was now twenty-one and clearly set on a course which would take me overseas. However, there was the question of marriage. For seven years I had been friends with a local boy who had already begun to fulfil his vocation in the church. But he was decidedly committed to the church at home, rather than overseas. So I felt it was time to discontinue the relationship. But even then I was conscious that there were other reasons for my decision. I recall one incident in particular. I had travelled to see him and we were returning from an outing together. As we entered the railway station he rushed ahead, bought his own ticket and left me to follow. Why, not only was he going to take away my independence but he could not even behave like a gentleman!

Missionary training took me to Bristol, England to read for a degree in theology and follow the course of study which would

qualify me for lay ministry in the Church of England. The college
took me once again into a woman's world, except that some of us
shared lectures with students from the men's colleges. Perhaps we
made the same mistake as some of the first women students at
Cambridge and allowed our names to appear at the top of the list,
more often than not. In any case I saw male chauvinism with a
vengeance. There were two men in particular who must have spent
a disproportionate part of their study time preparing awkward
questions to entrap a certain female lecturer (they failed their
finals!) and there was the small group of men who in those days
of gowned formality remained firmly in their seats when the rest
of us stood for prayer on the entrance of the same lecturer. And
there was the male lecturer who made snide remarks at the expense
of women whenever the occasion allowed. It was to be a portent
of things to come.

When, eventually, I arrived in Kenya, East Africa, as a
missionary teacher, it was to a mixed but generally positive recep-
tion – for I was a woman with theological expertise. A clergy wife
rather pointedly confided how her husband, if only he had had
the opportunity, could clearly have earned himself a theological
degree. The bishop when asked by one of his younger African
clergy if I might preach at the mother's day service agreed, with
the proviso that someone else should preach a short sermon first
from the pulpit and I should then speak from the chancel steps!
My local missionary vicar protested when I was asked to preach
from the pulpit of the neighbouring nonconformist church for the
Sunday service of the girls' secondary school. Apparently the
pulpit was the symbol of male privilege and authority. Why, I
argued, was it all right to teach future church leaders theology
while it was wrong to preach? African Christians, in my experience, made no distinction between the male 'white *mwalimu*
(teacher)' and the female variety: they accorded them equal
respect. And in ecumenical ventures which included mixing with
Roman Catholic priests, brothers and sisters as well as Protestant
clergy and laity I seemed to be accepted as a professional person
in my own right. Yet it was in Africa that I encountered situations
which led me to study anthropology and undertake a research

project which related directly to the position of women in society. As I worked among the Nandi and researched their rituals of initiation, marriage and divorce I could not help but become aware of the problems surrounding female circumcision, polygyny and the custom of bridewealth.[1]

When I returned to England to write up my research I was invited to set up a department of missiology in my old college – now merged with the men's. At first, all went well and I was given positions of responsibility. But alas, I lacked power. And as consciousness dawned I began to understand that whatever my age, experience or qualifications I was neither male nor ordained and consequently did not wield the same authority or command the same respect as my clerical colleagues. In addition I belonged to that other strange species: the unmarried. I was a second-class citizen on a journey to nowhere. And this was never brought home to me more forcefully than when I enquired about a change of job only to discover that I should have had to serve under a young man whom I had taught three years previously!

As I reached this point I became increasingly involved in the debates surrounding covenanting and the ordination of women, so I set out on a new journey of discovery. It is a journey which I invite you to share with me in the pages that follow. I examine the biblical teaching on the relationship between man and woman – their creation in the image of God and their oneness in Christ, survey the ministry of women in the church, explore the concerns of the women's movements past and present and map out a future for woman as a person and in relation with man, married and single, in the home and at work.

I hold passionately to two convictions on the subject: God made man and woman in relationship in his own image; in Christ there is no male and female – all are one in Christ Jesus.

Part Two:

LOOKING AT THE PAST

2: In God's Image
Man and Woman in the Old Testament

Christians, Muslims and Jews alike accord the Old Testament a unique and authoritative position in their respective doctrines of divine revelation. But this does not mean that it came full-blown from heaven, as it were, written by the finger of God on tablets of stone or plates of gold. Rather, it is anchored in history: it is the book of a particular people, albeit a peculiar people, God's chosen people of Israel. And it is the record of God's (Yahweh's) dealings with these people in history. Therefore it is at the same time both human and divine and contains human and divine elements.

More precisely it can be said that the Old Testament is not one book but a library of thirty-nine separate volumes based on very ancient traditions and taking literary form in the years between the tenth and second centuries BC. As literature it is very varied and includes myth, history, poetry, proverbs and prophecy. Consequently any attempt to understand the message of the Old Testament and apply its meaning for today must bear this diversity in mind.

The early Christians took over the canon of the Jewish Scriptures, adding to it later a canon of their own witnessing to the revelation of God and the new covenant in Jesus Christ.[1] For Christians, God's word in its primary sense is Christ himself, the *Logos* or living word. Yet the Old Testament is recognised as the inspired and authoritative word of God because it points forward to salvation through the Christ who was to come and the New Testament because it proclaims a Christ already arrived.

The Bible as a whole, when interpreted literally and traditionally on the relationship between man and woman, is both loved and hated. Fundamentalists love it and feminists hate it because on such a reading it appears to affirm the inferior status and subordinate role of woman. The fundamentalist, Larry Christenson, basing his views 'unashamedly on certain passages and principles written down in the Bible . . . as true and valid today as when they were written' outlines a 'divine order' or 'hierarchy' with Christ as head of the husband and lord of the family and the husband as head of the wife and chief authority over the children.[2] The feminists, Susan Dowell and Linda Hurcombe, tell how their own 'quest for a mature woman's respect for and understanding of the books which constitute the Bible is scored with pain and anger' and how 'as a history of religious consciousness the Bible traces in its narratives and its silences the secondary status of women.'[3] However, there is a much more satisfactory and authentic way of interpreting Old and New Testaments alike which leads to very different conclusions.

1. Cultural conditioning and biblical interpretation

We were a mixed group, ecumenical, multi-racial and belonging to both sexes, gathered round a table discussing new syllabuses in religious education for the secondary schools of East Africa. Somehow, the conversation got round to *matriarchy* (when mother rules as head of the family and descent is traced through the female line) and *patriarchy* (when father rules as head of the family and descent is traced through the male line). I shall never forget the expression of incredulity and dismay on the face of an African priest when he heard that such 'monstrosities' as matriarchal societies actually existed, even close at hand in East Africa!

Cheju Island lies off the coast of Korea. It is inhabited by about 60,000 people and until the influx of tourists in recent years had escaped outside influences for a considerable period of its history. Traditionally, in Cheju, the women worked for the family living while the men stayed at home and cared for the children. Korean society as a whole, conservative and patriarchal, prefers to publicise the matter as little as possible.

A student approached me, concerned at the reply which she had received from her Old Testament lecturer on her enquiry about the implications of certain so-called 'timeless' laws for matriarchal societies. The problem didn't arise, or so she was told, as God had clearly chosen the patriarchal order as the vehicle of his revelation. Thus, ignoring and depreciating cultural diversity, many Christian theologians make patriarchy absolute. Little wonder that women feel denigrated.

This said, however, there is much that is encouraging. For even conservatives nowadays stress the significance of cultural diversity and recognise the importance of acknowledging the relevance of cultural conditioning for interpreting the Bible:

> God's personal self-disclosure in the Bible was given in terms of the hearers' own culture. . . .
>
> The biblical writers made critical use of whatever cultural material was available to them for the expression of their message. For example, the Old Testament refers several times to the Babylonian sea monster named 'Leviathan', while the form of God's 'covenant' with his people resembles the ancient Hittite Suzerain's 'treaty' with his vassals. The writers also made incidental use of the conceptual imagery of the 'three-tiered' universe, though they did not thereby affirm a pre-Copernican cosmology. We do something similar when we talk about the sun 'rising' and 'setting'.
>
> Similarly, New Testament language and thought-forms are steeped in both Jewish and Hellenistic cultures, and Paul seems to have drawn from the vocabulary of Greek philosophy. . . .
>
> We have not been able to devote as much time as we would have liked to the problem of the cultural conditioning of Scripture. We are agreed that some biblical commands (e.g., regarding the veiling of women in public and washing one another's feet) refer to cultural customs now obsolete in many parts of the world. Faced by such texts, we believe the right response is neither a slavishly literal obedience nor an irresponsible disregard, but rather a critical discernment of the text's inner meaning and then a translation of it into our own culture. For example, the inner meaning of the command to

wash each other's feet is that mutual love must express itself in humble service. So in some cultures we may clean each other's shoes instead. We are clear that the purpose of such 'cultural transposition' is not to avoid obedience but rather to make it contemporary and authentic.[4]

It is the cultural conditioning associated with patriarchy as a social system which poses the greatest problems for understanding biblical teaching on woman and/or man-woman relationships today. Throughout the period of both testaments patriarchy was conceived as the God-given norm. However, as I intend to demonstrate, it is egalitarian and not patriarchal reality which God intended from the beginning. Biblical affirmations of the equality of man and woman established at creation and restored in Christ may be seen as *descriptive* of God's intention for Man (humankind), and the biblical injunctions for woman's subordination as *prescriptive* attempts to re-establish patriarchal reality, which is a culturally relative phenomenon.[5] Unfortunately, the latter are usually interpreted as descriptive, unchanging and binding for all time. A good parallel from Christian history is the absolutising of monarchy in the doctrine of the divine right of kings. Who today would wish to exalt monarchy above democracy and all other modes of government as God's will for all peoples?

2. Creation and fall: Genesis 1–3

The Old Testament presents us with two major creation narratives, the first, belonging to the priestly tradition, P (about the sixth century BC), in Genesis 1.1–2.4a, and the second, belonging to the Yahwist tradition (about the ninth century BC), in Genesis 2.4b–25 and a third celebratory hymn of creation in Psalm 8. The second creation account took its present literary form earlier than the first but it is most likely that the first is based on a more ancient tradition.[6]

Both accounts portray Man ('*adam*, collective and generic, 'humankind' or 'mankind') as the crown of God's creative achievement. In the first account, logical and concise in style but abstract in concept, Man is the apex of creation. By God's word heaven and earth, land and sea, plant life and heavenly lights, birds, fish and animals have come into being to his great satisfaction. Then God (*Elohim*) deliberates and decides as a fitting climax to his handiwork to make Man in his own image and likeness. In the second account, a beautifully told picture-story, vivid and concrete, Man occupies centre stage; he is the pivot of the story as in the first he was the climax. The Lord God (*Yahweh Elohim*) fashions Man of dust from the ground and, breathing into him, makes him a living being. He then proceeds to plant a garden for him to tend, to create living creatures for his comfort and enjoyment, and finally one of his own kind – woman – to be his true companion or helpmate.

The account of the fall follows, when woman and then man gives in to temptation and both are condemned and punished: the woman to bear her children in pain and to live in subordination to her husband, the man to till the soil with difficulty and die.

(i) In the image and likeness of God: Genesis 1.1–2:4a
In this passage the key verses relevant to the subject of the man-woman, male-female relationship are 1.26–28:

> Then God said, 'Let us make man in our image, after our likeness; and let them have dominion over the fish of the sea and over the birds of the air, and over the cattle, and over all the earth, and over every creeping thing that creeps upon the earth.' So God created man in his own image, in the image of God he created him; male and female he created them. And God blessed them, and God said to them, 'Be fruitful and multiply, and fill the earth and subdue it; and have dominion over the fish of the sea and over the birds of the air and over every living thing that moves upon the earth.'
>
> (Gen. 1.26–28, RSV)

Let us make Man, says God, by the plural pronoun either expressing his majesty or, more likely, deliberating within the complex organic nature of his own being.[7] And Man is made *in God's own image and likeness*. The Hebrew words, *tselem* and *demuth*, translated respectively as 'image' and 'likeness', are used in parallel but the latter also serves to modify the former. *Tselem* means predominantly an actual plastic work, a duplicate, sometimes an idol (1 Sam. 6.5) or a painting (Ezek. 23.14). To indicate their claim to dominion, kings placed images in their imperial provinces. *Demuth* means predominantly something abstract, an appearance, a similarity, an analogy (Ezek. 1:5, 10, 26, 28) but also a copy (2 Kings 16.10).[8] There are suggestions, therefore, of physical and spiritual correspondence between God and Man. The whole man is made in God's image and after his likeness; and the physical and spiritual must be split as little as possible. However, it is useful to identify the godlikeness of Man in the beauty and perfection of his physical form and in his spiritual powers of thought, communication and self-transcendence. By virtue of this correspondence, Man differs from the animals and is destined for a personal relationship with his Maker. But he is also destined to play an intermediary role in creation: he stands between God and the rest of his creatures. Man is *to have dominion . . . over all the earth*: such is the purpose of man's similarity to God, that he should rule the earth and subdue it as God's representative or steward. Then, perhaps most glorious of all, Man is created neither unisex (male or female) nor androgynous (male and female in one person) but with sexual duality and polarity as *male and female*. It is each sex in his or her own right and both together who reflect God's being and exercise dominion in the world. So, too, together they are blessed and exhorted to be fruitful in procreation and to subdue the earth to meet their needs.

According to the first account of creation, therefore, man and woman are equal: neither sex is inferior nor superior to the other. And as if to make no mistake about it Genesis 5.1–2 repeats the assertion: 'When God created man, he made him in the likeness of God. Male and female he created them, and he blessed them and named them Man when they were created.'

(ii) Two of a kind: Genesis 2.4b–25
The significant verses for our purposes in the second creation account are 2.7, 18–24:

> Then the Lord God formed man of dust from the ground, and breathed into his nostrils the breath of life; and man became a living being. . . . Then the Lord God said, It is not good that the man should be alone; I will make him a help fit for him. So out of the ground the Lord God formed every beast of the field and every bird of the air . . . but for the man there was not found a help fit for him. So the Lord God caused a deep sleep to fall upon the man, and while he slept took one of his ribs and closed up its place with flesh; and the rib which the Lord God had taken from the man he made into a woman and brought her to the man. Then the man said,
> > 'This at last is bone of my bones
> > and flesh of my flesh;
> > she shall be called Woman,
> > because she was taken out of Man.'
> Therefore a man leaves his father and his mother and cleaves to his wife, and they become one flesh.
>
> > (Gen. 2.7, 18–24, RSV)

The second creation account has been traditionally associated with the marriage relationship – perhaps because both Jesus and Paul alluded to it – and interpreted as portraying woman created *after* man, *from* man and *for* man. Thus is implied an inferior sex created as an 'afterthought' in order to be a 'helpmate' for the male. To my mind the interpretation is both unsatisfactory and naïve and probably owes its origin to an extreme literalism and a reading back into the text (perhaps from the Genesis account of the fall and the customs of patriarchal society).

The *priority argument* – which maintains that because the male was created first he is destined to be the dominant sex – is no argument at all. Compare, for example, the first and second creation accounts. In the first, Man's creation comes last of all; as the crown of creation he features as the climax of the story. In the second, Man is created first; he is central to the drama of creation. But he is incomplete without a partner of his own kind and so woman (perhaps potentially present in Man (still *'adam*)) is created at the end of the drama as the final act of God's creative activity.

The *derivative argument* – which maintains that because woman was made from a rib taken from man (a pun on the Hebrew, *'ishshah* from *'ish*) she is somehow his subordinate – must have little validity when one considers that man comes from the dust of the ground. Moreover, man is to leave his father and mother and cleave to his wife.

Similarly, the *helpmate argument* – which maintains that because woman was made to be man's companion or helpmate she is somehow his inferior – pays little attention to man's incompleteness without woman and the significance of the word translated 'helpmate'. As Joyce Baldwin so aptly points out: 'The word "help" (*ezer*) in no way suggests a subordinate. On the contrary, it is used in the Old Testament mainly of God who helps and delivers his people (Gen. 49.25; Exod. 18.4; Deut. 33.26). Perhaps the most familiar use of the word is in 1 Samuel 7.12, where Samuel sets up a memorial and calls it *Ebenezer*, "stone of help", because, he said, *Hitherto the Lord has helped us*. If the usage of the word "help" is any guide, therefore, the woman was meant to be in the privileged position of being a support and a blessing to the man.'[9]

That a husband should leave his father and mother and cleave to his wife, thus becoming one with her in sexual union, is the basis on which Jesus and the Christian Church has argued for life-long monogamous marriage. But for our purposes it is of great significance that, in a creation account committed to its present written form in a patriarchal society where it was the norm for a woman to leave her family to join her future husband's, the male is depicted as leaving his home to unite with the female.

According to the second creation account, therefore, man and woman as male and female are two of a kind: they are equal yet complementary. Moreover, they are made for what Martin Buber has taught us to call the 'I – Thou' relationship between two equal partners.

(iii) The fall from innocence: Genesis 3

So far as woman is concerned the problem with the biblical story of Man's fall is twofold: 1. Christian theology through the ages has blamed Man's loss of innocence and the marring of God's image and likeness primarily on the female of the species (now called Eve, the 'mother of all living') because it was she who first succumbed to temptation and proceeded, as 'Eve the temptress' to lead the male (now called Adam) astray; 2. the punishment meted out to woman includes sexual subordination to her husband, so disrupting the marriage relationship.

But the problem can be resolved for Christians today by the application of good scientific method using insights from theology, biology, psychology and social anthropology.

For those who would interpret human nature and the relation between the sexes in biological and psychological terms and who would see the role stereotypes in Genesis as belonging to patriarchal society, the soluton is easy and obvious: the male is off-loading his guilt on to the female and turning his male envy of the female procreative role into dominance.

For those who take the unfolding drama at face value and apply a sophisticated hermeneutic (method of biblical interpretation) and less fundamentalist theological perspective, the woman's pain in childbirth and the wife's sexual subordination parallel the man's expulsion from the garden and his condemnation to till the ground and eat bread with sweat on his brow until he returns to the dust from whence he came. As Gerhard von Rad and Derek Kidner, respectively, paint and interpret the picture: 'The woman's punishment struck at the deepest root of her being as wife and mother, the man's strikes at the innermost nerve of his life: his work, his activity, and provision for sustenance.'[11] 'The phrase *your desire shall be for your husband* (RSV), with the reciprocating *he shall rule over you*, portrays a marriage relation in which control has slipped from the fully personal realm to that of instinctive urges passive and active. "To love and to cherish" becomes "To desire and to dominate".'[12] But even then we must not forget that some aspects of the division of labour here described belong to certain types of social organisation, often patriarchal in character. To return to the

curse pronounced after the fall, the punishment of both man and
woman is to be reversed in God's act of redemption foreseen in
verse 15, when the Lord God declares enmity between the seed of
the serpent and the seed of the woman; here, we catch what Kidner
calls 'the first glimmer of the gospel'.[13] Certainly any literalist
reading of the Genesis stories of Man's creation and fall must
expect a restoration of God's image, as indeed Paul reminds us so
eloquently and so forcefully in his letter to the Christians in Rome:
'As man's [Greek *anthrōpos*, generic man] trespass led to condemnation for all men, so one man's act of righteousness leads to
acquittal and life for all men. For as by one man's disobedience
many were made sinners, so by one man's obedience many will
be made righteous' (Rom. 5.18, 19).

With the coming of Jesus the Messiah the restoring of the image
began and it continues today as the pain of childbirth is eased, the
slog of manual labour is reduced and woman is freed from sexual
oppression. The unity and solidarity between God and Man,
between male and female and between Man and his environment,
which because of sin had degenerated to disunity, diversity and
selfish individualism, is being restored in Christ.

3. Marriage and the family: woman in the home

A woman in Israel found her identity not as an individual but as
a member of a family – first as daughter, then as wife and finally
as mother. This was normal for patriarchal society. It is not surprising, therefore, that most Old Testament texts concerning woman
place her in the home as wife, mother and mistress of the household. The wisdom literature in particular sings her praises in all
three roles. *Conjugal love* is praised in the Song of Songs, as when
the lover says of her beloved, 'Your love is better than wine,' and
he replies, 'You are beautiful, my love' (Song 1.2, 15) and in the
book of Proverbs we are told, 'He who finds a wife finds a good
thing' (Prov. 18.22). We are informed, too, that Isaac loved
Rebecca (Gen. 24.67), Jacob loved Rachel (Gen. 29.18, 20),
Elkanah comforted the childless Hannah with his love (1 Sam. 1.8)
and Michal loved David (1 Sam. 18.20). Similarly, the *maternal role*

s prized from very ancient times: 'Honour your father and your
mother', commands the decalogue. One of the ways in which a
woman showed herself a good wife was to bear her husband children, especially sons, and nurture them (Prov. 31.1–9). To be
childless, particularly a childless widow (for a widow could not
even inherit her late husband's property), was pitiable in the
extreme. As mother, a woman had some say in selecting a future
daughter-in-law and dedicating her children to the service of God.
Mother-love even becomes a potent theme in Scripture. There are
many stories of mothers mourning their dead children (2 Sam.
21.7–14; 2 Kings 4.18–37) and the mother who tells Solomon that
she would rather give up her child than have it divided between
herself and the other claimant becomes a type of maternal altruism
(1 Kings 3.16–28). Eventually mother-love becomes a theme of
God's love for Israel. The Lord enquires of his people: 'Can a
woman forget her sucking child, that she should have no compassion on the son of her womb? Even these may forget, yet I will
not forget you' (Isa. 49.15) and again, 'As one whom his mother
comforts, so I will comfort you' (Isa. 66.13). And no praise is too
great for the 'good wife' and mistress of the household described
lyrically in Proverbs 31.10–31: she acquires and spins wool and
flax to weave the cloth and make the clothing for her family and
the market, burning her lamp into the night and rising before
dawn; she buys the land, plants the crops and provides food for
the household; in character she is strong, dignified and wise; her
husband trusts her and her children call her blessed. Such a woman
wielded an influence almost incalculable.[14]

Legally, however, a woman in Israel had very few rights: she
was more a chattel than a person, her position inferior to that of
woman in any of the great countries round about. In marriage she
passed from the dominion of her father to that of her husband to
whom he gave her in marriage (1 Sam. 18.17, 19, 27), having
negotiated a dowry. Polygamy was quite common and laid a heavy
burden on any wife, particularly if she did not enjoy the blessing
of children, consequently suffering the disdain and ridicule of
other wives and concubines. Fidelity was required of the woman
alone and this applied to the betrothed as well as the married. If

a married woman were suspected of adultery she had to underge 'trial by ordeal'. A man could divorce his wife but not a woman her husband. A husband had to be careful not to commit adultery against another woman's husband. In any event it was the woman who was most severely punished for infidelity (Deut. 24.1; Num. 5.11–31; Exod. 22.16; Deut. 22.22–29; Gen. 38.12–26). One of the few provisions for a woman's protection in this area of legisla tion was the grounds for divorce and the certificate provided (Deut 24.1). In the case of the levirate when, if a man died without son to inherit, the law permitted his brother to marry the widow, th brother might reject the new marriage but not the wife (Deut 25.5–10). In every respect, therefore, the husband was his wife' lord (*ba'al*) (Gen. 3.16). Israelite society was thoroughl patriarchal.

There were a few exceptions to these harsh laws: as when ther were no sons, and daughters could inherit (Num. 27.8) and in thes circumstances and on other occasions a girl might be consulted o marriage (Num. 36.6; Gen. 24.39, 58).[15] And later on in Israel' history there are indications of greater consideration for a wife' rights and concern for a husband's fidelity. Proverbs 5.15–19 an Malachi 2.15 exhort husbands to be faithful to their wives becaus it is the will of God. Hosea 4.13–14 makes clear that no doub standard applies at this stage in Israel's history: adultery is likene to idolatry and forbidden to men and women alike. The Aproc rypha goes one step further and speaks of a wife's adultery as firs of all disobedience to the law of God, next falsity to her husban and finally the bringer of shame on herself and on any illegitimat children she might bear (Ecclus. 23.22–27).

4. Discriminations, restrictions and taboos

Unlike neighbouring peoples, the Israelites did not admit wome to the priesthood. Two possible reasons are often put forward f the ban. First, women are associated with sorcery (Exod. 22.18 which the Deuteronomist calls 'an abomination to the Lord' (Deu 18.12). Second, and much more probably (but of course neithe precludes the other), women are associated with ritual impurity

While ritually unclean, women may not enter the sanctuary. A woman was unclean during her menstrual flow and for seven days afterwards (Lev. 15.19), while seminal emission made a man unclean only 'until the evening' (Lev. 15.16). After childbirth, when the child was male, a woman was considered unclean for seven days as at menstruation and after circumcision on the eighth day for thirty-three days more. For a female child the period of uncleanness was doubled (Lev. 12.1–8). After the time of purification was over the woman was required to bring an offering to the priest so that he could make atonement for her.

With respect to dietary and sacrificial regulations women and men appear to have been under the same obligations (for example, Lev. 11). However, although a woman could take the Nazirite vow of special consecration to the Lord, it was only with her male protector's consent, demonstrating how a woman was considered a minor all her life unless she was a widow or a divorcee (Num. 30). Similarly, although a wife might rest on the sabbath, she was not required to do so as were the husband, his sons and daughters, his menservants and maidservants, farm animals and even the sojourner within his gate (Exod. 20.8–11; Deut. 5.12–15).[16]

In earliest times the vow of persons involved human sacrifice. But Moses legislated instead for a valuation in cash and the values are listed in Leviticus 27. Suffice it to note here that woman is consistently valued at a lower rate than man; for example, a male aged between twenty and sixty years was valued at fifty shekels and a female of the same age at thirty shekels.

In earliest childhood boys and girls were educated by their mothers. But as they grew boys were turned over to their fathers for training in trades and crafts and instruction in their national and religious heritage. But the latter also involved training by prophets, priests and elders so that boys also learned the Torah (law) vital to the life of every male Israelite. Boys were educated for manhood as well as fatherhood, girls for wifehood and motherhood alone.

5. Professionals and charismatics: women outside the home

Certain professions were followed by women in Israel. We know of
women who were professional mourners (Jer. 9.17–22), midwives
(Gen. 35.17), temple singers (Ezra 2.65), and nurses (Ruth 4:16).
Some, too, were prostitutes, tolerated but without status, and
sorcerers, feared and hated as well as condemned (Deut. 18.9–14,
Exod. 22.18).

As so often in societies where they are barred from functioning
within the official religious and political structures, women in Israel
found their outlets elsewhere. If the priesthood and monarchy were
closed to them, charismatic office was not. So it is that the women
who most inspire us in the pages of the Old Testament are
prophetesses, judges and political leaders. Who has not heard of
Deborah, political leader and prophetess who, during the period
of the judges, saved the nation (Judg. 4–5); or of Huldah, the
prophetess who, during the time of the kings, played an important
part in public affairs (2 Kings 22.14–20); or of Esther, beautiful
and courageous queen who, during Israel's exile, championed the
cause of her people (Esther)? Time does not permit me to tell of
Tamar, Miriam, Rahab, Jael, Ruth, Naomi, Hannah, Jehosheba
and countless others who by patience, cunning and daring played
their part in Israel's history.

Conclusions

At creation woman is depicted as made in the image and likeness
of God, man's complement and equal. At the fall she is condemned
to pain in childbirth and subordination to her husband in the
marriage relationship. In patriarchal Israelite society she is mostly
portrayed as male property, in the roles of mother, wife and
daughter; only widows and divorcees escape the restrictions which
ownership imposes. Towards the end of the Old Testament period,
however, woman appears to be gaining in personhood, even in her
role as a wife. And from time to time woman holds charismatic
office without, apparently, suffering any denigration or discrimination on account of her sex and gender.

3: One in Christ

Authority in the relationship between man and woman in the New Testament

The New Testament, like the Old, as is readily acknowledged by contemporary scholars, is a complex set of documents comprising a diverse collection of literary pieces by several different authors and representing a variety of theological perspectives. And in order to come to a satisfactory conclusion on its teaching concerning 'authority' in the relationship between man and woman, the scholar and exegete is obliged to do one of (at least) three things: to let certain texts speak for themselves while suppressing others or at the least re-interpreting them out of context; to allow the obvious contradictions to remain; or, as I prefer, to take every text in context and in relation and grapple with what I perceive to be fundamental agreement in the face of tension and development. On the one hand the message of the Gospels and of Paul (on certain occasions) is clear: in Christ there is no male and female – there is equality between the sexes. On the other hand the militant and insensitive assertion of these new-found rights and freedoms poses a threat to the ecclesiastical and social order.

In an attempt to resolve this tension, Christians resorted to applying rabbinic exegesis and interpretation of Old Testament texts (especially those recounting creation and fall in Genesis) in order to play down equality in the interest of cultural sensitivity and social harmony. After all, the young church was a minority movement fighting for survival in a hostile environment. To step out of line would have been to invite violent suppression.

My thesis is a simple one. Yet because of the vast quantity of material and the voluminous amount of writing on the subject I

37

cannot hope to do it justice or fully state and defend my case.
can but try. . . .

1. The cultural and religious background

As we peruse the New Testament and consider its social and
cultural background it becomes obvious that the key issue with
which we must concern ourselves is the place accorded woman in
the contemporary world. Man's place is assured, then as now: as
one writer tellingly remarks, in any index the occurrence o
'WOMAN – position of' is normal, while man needs no such
reference!

Characteristic of the traditional position and estimation o
woman is a saying current in different forms among the Persians
Greeks and Jews, in which man gives thanks that he is not an
unbeliever or uncivilised, that he is not a woman and that he i
not a slave.[1] A form of the saying was carried over into synagogu
worship and is still to be found today in the Jewish prayer book
with the consoling addition for the woman that she is made accor
ding to God's will.[2] Significantly, as we shall come to see, not only
the substance of such sentiment but the actual order and form in
which it was expressed underlies much of Paul's teaching on
authority in the relationship between man and woman.

(i) Greece

In Athens and ancient Greece generally woman was reckoned to
be of an inferior kind. She was to be guarded by dogs in separate
quarters; she was fickle, contentious and nature's greatest misfi
with no claim to culture. Her normal fate was to be despised and
oppressed, especially if she did not enjoy male protection.[3]
household in which she had the final say would ultimately perish.

But there were other points of view. Macedonia and the ancien
state of Sparta stand out as being exemplary in granting high
status and freedom of opportunity to woman. And many Athenian
deeply loved and respected their wives, 'honouring them as mother
of their children and managers of their homes'.[5] Then, a certai
ambivalence is to be detected among the poets and philosophers

Demosthenes summed up the three major classes of Greece in his now famous remark: 'We have *hetairai* for the pleasures of the spirit, concubines for sensual pleasure and wives to give us sons'.[6] Wives were secluded and closely guarded, regarded as permanent minors and controlled by a guardian – father, husband, husband's heir, or even the state. And as a man thus found it improper to take out his wife in public he resorted to an *hetaira* (a 'companion', 'girl friend' or 'mistress') who was artistic, cultured, often well-educated and perhaps even an intellectual. The *hetairai* were treated essentially as equals and often earned their living by engaging in commerce in the Greek cities. One can imagine some of the women mentioned in the New Testament in this category. The concubines were temporary replacements for wives who were ill, pregnant or recovering from childbirth.[7] And as elsewhere women served also as prostitutes (both religious and secular), slaves and street-walkers. Commentators differ in the interpretation of Plato's attitude to woman: some see him as moving in the direction of accepting a basic similarity between the natures of man and woman so that he could recommend the education of woman. Others see his concession as being utilitarian and not fundamental. However, there is little doubt about Aristotle's stance. Man and woman are by nature ordained for different functions, man being strong in body and mind and woman weak and delicate in constitution.[8] But even more strongly he adds: 'For females are weaker and colder in nature and we must look upon the female character as being a sort of natural deficiency.' And again: 'The first and least parts of a family are master and slave, husband and wife, father and children'; 'A husband and father rules over wife and children'; 'The male is by nature fitter for command than the female'; 'The courage of a man is shown in commanding, of a woman in obeying'.[9] A key to understanding Aristotle's tendency to relegate much of humanity to sub-human status is his concept of 'rule' which he finds throughout nature: some are destined to rule, others to be ruled – as is obvious both from reason and experience. Of immense consequence to medieval Christian theology and misogyny in the church is the fact that Thomas Aquinas 'the angelic doctor' developed the Aristotelian position.

Divorce was not uncommon and was enacted in several ways: by common consent of both parties, by the unilateral action of either, by simple declaration before a judge or even through a third party. Repeated divorce led to a form of successive polygamy.[10]

(ii) Rome

Woman fared generally better in Rome. Marriage was monogamous and in the household the husband had only a mild superiority which constantly diminished. Woman moved about freely, accompanying her husband to the theatre, races and other forms of public entertainment. And some Stoics even debated the possibility of education for woman. Divorce was possible by mutual repudiation but often became easy for a man with his rise in social class or his desire for another woman. Moreover, while a woman was required to be sexually chaste, a man was not and a woman was as a rule subject to father and husband as was evidenced by a father's 'right' to arrange his daughter's marriage and command her consent.[11]

Generally speaking, therefore, while Roman woman might be relatively liberated only the man had the right to be always and unquestioningly so by the law of nature.

(iii) Judaism

By the time of Jesus, many of the rights accorded woman in the late Old Testament and intertestamental periods had been eroded. In Judaism, therefore, woman was more than ever part of a strong patriarchal society undergirded by a religious world view or 'sacred canopy' also decidedly patriarchal. In order to clarify, some recapitulation as well as expansion is called for. Legally, a woman was more a chattel than a person. In marriage she passed from the dominion of her father to her husband who, incidentally, might have other wives; she is also subject to the custom of the levirate which the man could reject but which she might not. Divorce was initiated by the man alone, being traditionally allowed only on account of unchastity. By the time of Jesus the schools of Shammai and Hillel disagreed on the proper grounds for divorce, the former allowing it for unchastity (the 'indecency' of Deut. 24.1) only and

he latter condoning it for anything from putting salt in the food
r burning a meal to desiring a more beautiful woman.

Woman was openly despised: 'Happy is he whose children are
males, and woe to him whose children are females.' Woman was
ot allowed to go out unveiled in public or to speak to man. One
f the oldest of sages wrote: 'Talk not much with womankind' to
vhich was added, 'They said this of a man's own wife: how much
nore of his fellow's wife?' Rules of propriety forbade a man to be
lone with a woman, to look at a married woman, or even to give
er a greeting. Indeed, in general it was considered preferable for
 woman, and especially an unmarried girl, not to go out at all.
Voman's education was limited to learning the domestic arts,
specially needlework and weaving and looking after the smaller
rothers and sisters.[12] She was in no circumstances to be taught
he Torah: 'May the words of the Torah be burned, they should
ot be handed over to a woman.'[13] Of course there were exceptions.

Finally, it was men and not women who counted to make up
he quorum of ten males (*minyan*) for a synagogue while women
rayed in a place apart (perhaps even in a gallery) and during the
me of Herod's temple could not proceed beyond the Court of the
entiles and Women. And during the time of menstruation and for
orty days after childbirth even these 'concessions' were removed.

And although certain of these rules were not kept among upper-
lass families the general attitude is well illustrated in the formula
Women, (Gentile) slaves and children (minors)'.[14]

. Woman in the life of Jesus

or a Jew and a Rabbi of his time Jesus' attitude to woman was
evolutionary both in precept and example.

) *Example*

esus appears to have no 'problem' in relation to the status and
osition of woman. All four Gospels depict his relationship with
oman as easy and natural. He allows women to touch him,
ccompany him, serve him and listen to his teaching.

At the well of Samaria he allows a sinful Samaritan woman

(thrice an outsider!) to give him a drink and converse with him (John 4.1–42). No wonder that both the woman and the returning disciples are amazed and possibly shocked (John 4.9, 27).

In the thick of the crowd he calls out to the woman with a haemorrhage who touched him and reassures her, reacting neither to her condition nor to his own consequent ritual impurity (Mark 5.21–43).

In the border region of Tyre and Sidon he encourages a Gentile woman to plead the case for her daughter's healing and commends her for her tenacity and wit (Mark 7.24–30).

In the house of Mary and Martha at Bethany he commends Mary who sits at his feet (in the posture of a student at the feet of a rabbi) for 'choosing the better part' and chides her sister Martha for being over-anxious with domestic affairs (Luke 10.38–42). Far from saying that 'a woman's place is in the home' Jesus speaks his only rebuke to a woman who is being 'the busy housewife'.[15]

In the house of Simon the Pharisee he allows a sinful woman to wet his feet with her tears, wipe them with her hair and anoint them with precious ointment (Luke 7.36–50).

At the resurrection he appears first to the women and commissions them to announce the good news to his disciples (Matt. 28.1–10 and parallels).

(ii) Teaching

Except for a couple of instances Jesus does not explicitly deal with the question of woman's status or position. He does not parallel his manner and behaviour with his teaching. However, he does allude to woman in his parables just as naturally as to man and distinctly more frequently than do the rabbis. There is, for example, the woman in search of a lost coin (Luke 15.8–10), the importunate widow asking for justice (Luke 18.1–8) and the ten maidens awaiting the bridegroom (Matt. 25.1–13).

It is seldom realised that in Jesus' teaching on divorce he is primarily questioning both the law of Moses and Jewish custom on the subject (Mark 10.1–12 and parallels). He takes issue with those who treat the woman as a chattel and gives her back her dignity as a person, appealing for support to the two accounts of creation in Genesis. First, he appeals to the creation of Man as male and female (Gen. 1.27) and then to the obligation on the man to leave his father and mother and to cling to his wife so that the two may be one (Gen. 2.24). If Jesus were applying the norms of a patriarchal society, where the woman leaves her family to join the man's he would not have put the onus on the man as he does here. Moreover, when he says that the man commits adultery against his wife (Mark 10.11) he is departing from the rabbis, who recognised adultery as being committed only against the husband (of the woman in question).

The debate about the Matthean exception clause is irrelevant for our purposes.

Similarly, in his teaching in the Sermon on the Mount, he exalts the status of woman when he equates adultery with 'looking at a woman lustfully'. The school of Hillel may have allowed a man to divorce his wife so that he could marry 'the latest attraction' but Jesus considered the very look in her direction as adulterous (Matt. 5.27–8).

Jesus thus removes the 'authority' which a man has over his wife: misunderstood and misused 'authority' which treated woman as a piece of property. (It is interesting to recall that even the decalogue – unsurpassed as a moral code for its time – forbids a man to covet, among other of his goods, his neighbour's wife!)

(iii) Jesus and Authority

From the time of his temptation in the desert when he refused worldly power, Jesus, by precept and example, affirms the priority of 'servanthood' over 'lordliness' in the messianic community. He who would be great must be least, he who would be first, last, and he who would rule must serve. Authority structures in the kingdom are to be a radical reversal of the world's. And when Jesus speaks out about 'power' he criticises synagogue and state alike:

> You are not to be called rabbi, for you have one teacher,
>   and you are all [brothers and sisters] brethren.

And call no man your father on earth, for you have one Father,
who is in heaven.
Neither be called masters, for you have one master,
the Christ.
He who is greatest among you shall be your servant.

(Matt. 23.8–11, RSV)

You know that the rulers of the Gentiles lord it over them,
and their great men exercise authority over them. It shall not
be so among you; but whoever would be great among you must
be your servant, and whoever would be first among you must
be your slave; even as the Son of Man came not to be served
but to serve, and to give his life as a ransom for many.

(Matt. 20.25–7, RSV)

The church has not always taken heed.[16]

3. Woman in the New Testament church

The eschatological hope was very much alive in the New Testament church: it dominated the motivation for mission in the Acts
(the end time which had been inaugurated was the age of the
Spirit) and dictated the agenda for many of Paul's letters. The
coming of the Lord was drawing near. And the new age, the age
of the Spirit, was to be an age when all, from the least to the
greatest, would love the Lord (Jer. 31.31–4) and sons and daughters would prophesy (Joel 2.28–9). Before and during the time of
Christ Jewish proselyte initiation required three things from man:
circumcision, baptism and sacrifice; but only two from woman:
baptism and sacrifice.[17] Already before Christ John the Baptist had
called men and women alike to the baptism of repentance in
preparation for the coming of God's kingdom. Hope abounded in
anticipation of the age of the Spirit when all sorts of contradictions
would be put right: the poor and lowly would be exalted, the
captives would be set free, the blind would recover their sight and
the oppressed would receive their liberty (Luke 1.46–55; 4.18,
19).[18] And Christian baptism which did not require circumcision

seemed to signal the fulfilment of that hope, as, for the first time, men and women alike became full initiates. There was no distinction in Christ, no male and female, all alike were full members of the new community. Imagine the liberation felt by women as the priesthood became a priesthood of all believers! The implications for church order and family relationship were enormous.

The picture of the church which we receive from the Acts and the Epistles indicates that women began to take full advantage of their new status. Nevertheless, as we examine the picture, two background factors need to be borne in mind: 1. There was precedent for certain liberties in Greco-Roman society as well as among upper class Jews; for example, when Paul visited Philippi (in Macedonia, already well-known for granting its women more freedom and prominence than elsewhere in the Greco-Roman world) he spoke to the women gathered for prayer at the riverside and Lydia and her household were baptised. 2. There are indications that women's behaviour in churches, for example, in Corinth, reveals symptoms of a spirit-possession movement arising from their marginal status in society at large; such movements are often fuelled by rapid and unsettling social change.[19]

Briefly, women were witnesses to the resurrection and were commissioned by the resurrected Lord to tell others. They fulfilled the credentials of apostleship and it is much more natural (in Rom. 16.7) to read Junia as a female name than to understand it as a shortened form of the male, Junianus. Andronicus and Junia would then appear as a missionary couple like Aquila and Priscilla.

Luke leaves us in no doubt that the Spirit of prophecy was given to women as well as men (Acts 2.17f.); he specifically mentions the four daughters of Philip as renowned Christian prophets (Acts 21.9). Even in 1 Corinthians chapters 11 to 14 Paul takes it for granted that women prophesied and performed liturgical functions; what he requests of them is that they exercise their gifts in an orderly manner. And whatever we may think of the woman 'Jezebel' there is no doubt but that she headed a prophetic school at Thyatira in the first century (Rev. 2.20ff.).

Again, Luke and Paul make it clear that women engaged in

missionary work and exercised leadership in the early church.
Women were among the wealthy and prominent converts and
patronesses (Acts 17.4, 12) and must have exercised leadership in
the house churches. Many house churches are associated with the
names of women: Apphia in Colossae (Philemon 2), Nympha in
Laodicea (Col. 4.15), Prisca and Aquila in Corinth, Ephesus and
Rome (1 Cor. 16.19; Acts 18: 18; Rom. 16: 5) and Chloe in Corinth
(1 Cor. 1.11). Paul commended the mission labours of women like
Mary, Tryphaena, Tryphosa and Persis in Rome (Rom. 16.6, 12)
and Euodia and Syntyche in Philippi (Phil. 4.2–3). Phoebe of
Cenchreae was called a deacon/deaconess and leader (Rom. 16.1)[20]
and Prisca (together with her husband) was a commissary of Paul,
Barnabas, Titus and Apollos – since her name is mentioned before
her husband's four times out of six she must have been the leading
figure.

In its setting, such evidence of woman's position in the church
is overwhelming and must not be allowed to be interpreted as
anything other than what it is: equal opportunities for women in
the life and witness of the earliest Christian communities. They
were full initiates and leaders as well as followers. However, we
do not know enough to comment on male/female relationships in
the working out of their respective roles and the interplay of the
sexes.

4. The magna carta of Christian liberty: Galatians 3.28

Galatians, as two authors put it, is Paul's 'freedom manifesto'.[21]
Elsewhere, too, Paul states forcefully 'the faith principle' but never
so much as a matter of life and death for the young community
as in his letter to the Christians of Galatia, where the truth of the
gospel appears to be at stake (Gal. 2.14): 'A man is not justified
by works of the law but through faith in Jesus Christ' (Gal. 2.16).
'For freedom Christ has set us free' he proclaims, and there is no
question of submitting again to circumcision which is nothing
other than 'a yoke of slavery' (Gal. 5.1).

In the midst of this manifesto occurs the claim (often called 'the
magna carta of Christian liberty') that as many as have been

baptised into Christ have put on Christ and are through faith 'sons of God' and 'Abraham's offspring', for 'there is neither Jew nor Greek, there is neither slave nor free, there is neither male nor female; for you are all one in Christ Jesus' (Gal. 3.27–9). Christian baptism does not require circumcision either to precede it or complete it: it is complete in itself.

There is a growing consensus among scholars that Galatians 3.28 represents a pre-Pauline baptismal formula. According to Hans Dieter Betz verses 26–28 stand apart in their formality of composition and structure; moreover, parallels in other literature suggest 'a form of a saying, made up of a number of components, which must have had its place and function in early Christian baptismal liturgy'.[22] Analysis reveals a six-line section as follows:

v.26 (1) For you are all sons of God, through [the] faith, in Christ Jesus.
v.27 (2) For as many of you as were baptised into Christ have put on Christ.
v.28a (3) There is neither Jew nor Greek;
v.28b (4) there is neither slave nor freeman;
v.28c (5) there is no male and female.
v.28d (6) For you are all one in Christ Jesus.

(Gal. 3.26–8)

There are two other close parallels in the New Testament: 1 Corinthians 12.13 and Colossians 3.11. In both instances 'baptism' or 'the putting on of the new man' is in mind and the opposites 'Jews/Greeks', 'slaves/freemen'; 'Greek/Jew', 'circumcised/uncircumcised', 'barbarian/Scythian' and 'slave/freeman' occur. In one of the Nag Hammadi Codices the opposites male/female and angel/man occur and later Christian liturgies contain statements similar to the passage from Galatians.

In verse 28 the parallel statements define the religious, cultural and social consequences of Christian baptismal initiation. The old status is named and by implication a new status is claimed.[23] Indeed, the language may be what is called 'performative language'; 'It is' says Betz 'significant that Paul makes these statements not as utopian ideals or as ethical demands, but as accomplished facts.'[24]

The first of the parallel statements declares that all distinctions between Jews and Greeks are abolished. Who today would deny that this involves cultural, social and political distinctions as well as religious? Hitherto both Jews and Greeks had held to the superiority of their respective race. But now Jews are liberated and Greeks are liberated – there is one race, in Christ. The second statement declares the institution of slavery abolished in Christ (and consequently in the community of the church entered by baptism). But throughout the ages this statement has been understood not only as abolishing the institution but also as declaring the institution of slavery irrelevant. It seems to me that Paul's views on the practical outworkings of the matter cannot always be harmonised (1 Cor. 7.21–4, 1 Cor. 12.13 and Philemon allow us to see outworkings of the principle in varying social contexts). The tiny threatened Christian community could not afford to challenge radically the whole social fabric and opted instead for 'equality' in the Christian community (at first!) and 'equality in Christ' but with social conformity outside it where necessary.[25] Yet the force of the charter remained and led eventually to the abolition of slavery in the nineteenth century. As early slaves like Onesimus felt the liberating force of the formula at their baptism so, too, did the negroes and Africans of the nineteenth and twentieth centuries. As with the second statement, so with the third – 'there is no male and female'. There has been disagreement about its implications, through the centuries, but there is no doubt about its plain meaning that in Christ and therefore in the Christian church sex distinctions between man and woman lose their significance. Galatians 3.28 is the first occurrence in antiquity of a doctrine openly propagating the abolition of sex distinctions. Surely the force of the statement for its time must have led to expressions of freedom among women parallel to those recorded among slaves (for example, Onesimus). But again, society could not take it and 'equality in Christ' was stressed so that the implications of the principle of the charter both for family and social life were not pressed home. It was not long before woman's behaviour was modified in the Christian community itself.[26]

It perhaps remains to be said that in Galatians 3.28 Paul the apostle of Christian liberty prevails over Paul the Jewish rabbi.

5. Paul to the Corinthians

Nobody reading Paul's correspondence with the church at Corinth and placing what he says in context can doubt that he had some tricky situations to deal with. Enthusiastic liberated Christians, men and women alike, were in danger of making excess the norm. And anybody with experience of worship and practice in 'charismatic' churches in the West today or in the 'independent' churches of Africa can readily discern the parallels.

(i) *1 Corinthians 7.3–5; 7.10–11*

When we consider Jean Héring's opinion that the seventh chapter of Paul's first letter to the Corinthians is 'the most important in the entire Bible for the question of marriage and related subjects' it is strange to notice to what extent it is almost universally ignored in the discussions of marriage and divorce and the relationship between man and woman.[27]

1 Corinthians 7.4 contains one of the two explicit references to 'authority' (*exousia*) in the passages under consideration. Answering queries from the Corinthians presumably relating to 'spiritual marriages' Paul recommends that each man should have his own wife and each woman her own husband. Each should give to the other his or her conjugal rights: 'For the wife does not rule over her own body, but the husband does; likewise the husband does not rule over his own body, but the wife does.' Moreover, refusal of conjugal rights is to be by agreement and only for a time for the purposes of prayer. The verb translated 'rule over' (*exousiazein*) indicates 'the right or power for something or over someone' or 'the right or power to do with something as one sees fit'. It is of considerable significance that Paul does not countenance either husband or wife 'lording it over' the other but admonishes each to allow the other rights over his or her body. The

relationship is to be one of mutual submissiveness, a relationship generally encouraged in Christ. Paul Jewett in his exposition of Genesis 1.27 makes much of the complementary nature of the sexes, seeing God as creating Man after his own image in relationship, the relationship in this instance being between male and female in an 'I – Thou' distinction of the sexes.[28] It seems to me enormously significant that in the 'I – Thou' of sexual intercourse when man and woman meet in all their 'distinctiveness' and 'oneness' ('difference' and 'sameness') that Paul assumes the equality of mutual submission. How different from the usual practice in a variety of cultures throughout the ages where woman has had few rights in the face of polygyny, prostitution and the threat of rape. Moreover, Paul's next admonition is revolutionary for its time: 'Do not refuse one another except perhaps by agreement for a season, that you may devote yourselves to prayer.' No male Jew wishing to withdraw for a period of prayer was obliged to seek the agreement of his wife. His was the prerogative both of prayer and of the freedom to engage in it. Comments F. F. Bruce: 'One-sided insistence on abstinence therefore amounts to robbing the other party of his or her rights.'[29]

With reference to 1 Corinthians 7.10–11 it is perhaps important to comment that Paul is in agreement with Jesus rather than with the schools of Jewish law on the matter of divorce. He appeals 'to the Lord' at this juncture having in mind perhaps a dominical saying on divorce such as that recorded in Mark 10. It is probably not too much to conjecture that when he asserts 'I give charge, not I but the Lord' he is conceding his own derived authority. Commenting on this passage Hans Conzelmann usefully reminds us of the contrast between divorce customs of the time and the teaching of Jesus, here enunciated by Paul:

> In the Jewish law of divorce, the rights of the wife are limited in the extreme. In Greek law, divorce is possible at the instigation of the husband, by common agreement, or at the instigation of the wife. The authentication of the divorce by an official authority is not necessary, only its registration. In Rome, too, divorce is freely allowed.[30]

'Wife' and 'husband' are in turn given priority of reference in the text and there is probably no reason to distinguish between the two Greek words translated 'separate' and 'divorce', as they appear to be used interchangeably.[31]

(ii) 1 Corinthians 11.2–16

Unfortunately in this chapter there is no time to discuss the niceties and details either of Paul's teaching or the numerous commentators' exegeses of this passage.

Paul's argument may be paraphrased as follows. Because the head of man is Christ, the head of woman is her husband and the head of Christ is God, so a man must not pray with his head covered (or he dishonours his head) and a woman must not pray or prophesy with her head uncovered (or she dishonours her head). A man ought not to cover his head, since he is the image and glory of God but woman is the glory of man. (For man was not made for woman, but woman for man.) That is why a woman ought to have a veil on her head, because of the angels. (But in the Lord neither is independent of the other, for as woman was made for man, so man is now born of woman. And all things are from God.) Nature itself teaches that it is degrading for a man to wear long hair but for woman it is her pride. This is the recognised practice of the churches. (Note – not a command of the Lord!)

The occasion is easily imagined: liberated women praying, prophesying and declaring their equality by worshipping without the veil. Why bother when marriages were 'spiritual' and the Lord was about to come? A first century Jewess was normally required to cover her face and her head in public; if she went out without this headdress her husband had the right – indeed the duty – to put her away without paying the divorce settlement.[32]

The passage is fraught with difficulties of interpretation; but fortunately most are irrelevant for our purposes. To my mind Paul allows women to prophesy but asks that the women prophets show due respect for the accepted order. The prior creation of the male in Genesis 2 is appealed to for support (normal in rabbinic exegesis) but Paul himself displays a certain amount of uncertainty when he concedes (almost as a logical afterthought) that man is born of

woman. Consequently, what I believe we have before us is a piece
of rabbinic exegesis employed to support Paul's arguments for
order in the congregation, an order which was to reflect the
accepted order of the day. It is dangerous to turn Paul's supporting
argument from rabbinic exegesis into a timeless principle. And
does nature so obviously teach us that man's hair must be short
and woman's long? Conservatives have been happy in recent years
to waive Paul's prescriptions for behaviour, allowing their women
to pray with uncovered head and bobbed hair. Instead they have
made Paul's supporting arguments into a timeless principle of the
subordination of female to male. If there is any timeless principle
to be learned from the passage it is cultural sensitivity and social
harmony.[33]

(iii) 1 Corinthians 14.33–6

For most commentators there is an obvious contradiction between
what Paul concedes in 1 Corinthians 11.2–16 with regard to
woman's right to prophesy and his apparent condemnation of the
practice in 1 Corinthians 14.33–6. The most common solution
offered is the view that the latter is an interpolation. On textual
grounds the interpolation is hardly justified and we must honestly
admit difficulty in understanding the mind of Paul. Nevertheless,
many suggestions have been made, not all of them improbable.
There is no time here to discuss these, but I have no doubt that,
whatever the basis for Paul's viewpoint, his concern once again is
order in the congregation. Prophecy and speaking in tongues are
common among women (and men) in ecstatic religious movements
and it is more than likely that the young church is at a loss as to
how to cope. To appeal to the norms of social and religious practice
elsewhere must have seemed eminently reasonable, if not a last
resort.

6. The household codes of Colossians, Ephesians, 1 Peter and the Pastorals

The household codes of the New Testament – *Haustafeln* – were
probably compact pieces of Christian instruction given orally in

the early Christian communities.[34] They have their pagan proto-
types, and since comparable material is to be found in, for example,
Philo and Josephus, many scholars claim that Hellenistic Judaism
borrowed this scheme of ethical instruction from popular philosophy, modified it slightly and used it in the synagogue.[35] In a
comparison of the types it has been claimed that the outstanding
Christian innovation is the emphasis on the reciprocal nature of
the obligations. Not only does a husband have rights over his wife
and children but he also has duties towards them. Nonetheless,
C. F. D. Moule can write: 'All said and done, however, the
greatest distinctiveness of the Christian ethical teaching lies not in
its contents so much as in its motives, its quality and its conditions:
        is *the* new factor.'[36] There is much to be said for both
points of view and I believe them to be complementary, as we
shall see in due course.

(i) Colossians 3.18–4.1; Ephesians 5.21–33

As elsewhere, in the household codes in Colossians and Ephesians,
the traditional patriarchal social order is reaffirmed, not just for
secular society but for the family and the Christian community.
Says Rosemary Radford Ruether in her discussion of the relation
of the 'religion of the sacred canopy' (the sacralisation of the
existing social order, patriarchy) to its prophetic critique:

> In the household codes of the New Testament the traditional
> patriarchal social order is reaffirmed, not simply for secular
> society, but for the Christian community. The dicta that children
> are to obey their parents, wives their husbands and slaves their
> masters is reiterated in no fewer than five places in the New
> Testament: Ephesians, Colossians, 1 Timothy, Titus and 1
> Peter. It is not accidental that three groups of dependants are
> mentioned in sequence in these codes. Women, children and
> slaves represent the three groups of dependants within the
> patriarchal *familia* of both Hebrew and Greco-Roman society.
> All are subjugated to the same Lord; namely, the male,
> property-owning head of family.[37]

And for a general introduction to and interpretation of these codes
few can better G. B. Caird. Let him say far more elegantly and
succinctly what I would wish to say (with some minor
reservations):

> Modern readers may feel a sense of disappointment that Paul's
> lofty ethical principles should prove to be reducible to such
> humdrum instructions, and may find it hard to square this
> passage with the sweeping declaration that in Christ 'there is
> neither slave nor free, there is neither male nor female' (Gal.
> 3.28). The mistake is to suppose that Paul is enunciating laws
> to govern Christian society for all time. Has he not constantly
> proclaimed himself the enemy of all such unbending legalism?
> And has he not in the previous paragraph spoken of a constant
> renewal of the Christian which should lead him into ever deeper
> appreciation of God's nature and will? Paul is a man of the mid
> first century advising his contemporaries how best they may
> apply their new faith to the social conditions of their day, and
> specifically to the family as they knew it. Jew and Gentile alike
> assumed that the head of a household would wield an authority
> which others were bound to obey. Paul does not openly
> challenge this assumption, but he modifies both the authority
> and its acceptance by the Christian principle of mutual love
> and deference, so that both are transformed.[38]

Several things may be said by way of comment and exegesis on
the Colossians and Ephesians passages.

The general rule in the New Testament church is mutual subordination or submissiveness, each member showing more concern
for the needs and rights of others than for his own. This is out of
reverence for Christ (Eph. 5.21).

Between wife and husband, child and parent, slave and master
there is to be a hierarchy of submission. However, if a wife is to
be submissive (*hupotassesthai*) to her husband, as the church is to
Christ, then he is to love (*agapan*) as Christ also loves the church;
and if a child is to obey his father then the father is to refrain
from being harsh or nagging to his child; similarly if slaves are

to obey their masters then the masters must forbear threatening behaviour, for there is one Master or Lord in heaven. The operative and qualifying phrase is the motive: 'as is fitting in the Lord' in Colossians and 'as to the Lord' in Ephesians. Following the codes thus becomes a means of pleasing the Lord, the truly submissive one, who was obedient to death, even death on a cross, and afterwards exalted as Lord of all (Phil. 2.5–11).

So Paul once again tries to keep 'oneness' or 'equality' in Christ and yet maintain social harmony.

Neither here nor in Galatians 3.28 can I see any justification for subsequent and contemporary Christian tendencies to divorce the man/woman issue from that of slavery. If the subordination of woman to man is a timeless principle (on this argument) then so also is the right of a man to enslave another.

To submit in the Lord as occasion demands is for Paul the true expression of a Christian's relationship with his Lord and of servanthood (but not servility) within the community. I see parallels with Paul's teaching on the 'strong' and the 'weak' conscience in 1 Corinthians 8 and his principle of 'being all things to all men' in 1 Corinthians 9. As a missionary in Africa, grappling with the living out of the gospel in a very different culture from my own in the West, these passages became very meaningful and relevant. Eight years of such experience have left an indelible mark on my hermeneutic.

(ii) 1 Peter 2.11–3.7; 1 Timothy 2.8–15; Titus 2.1–10

In these passages also wives are urged to be submissive to their husbands with due decorum. In the matter of who should exercise authority over whom the church has travelled further along the road towards conforming to the norms of society and Jewish paranesis.

The most explicit and problematic of the injunctions (for our purposes) is 1 Timothy 2.11–12 where the author says: 'Let a woman learn in silence with all submissiveness. I permit no woman to teach or to have authority over men; she is to keep silent.' Women must not be 'domineering' (*authentein*) over their menfolk, interrupting them while they are speaking in church; instead they must keep silence in all 'submissiveness' (*hupotagē*). The reason offered is that Adam was formed first, then Eve and it was woman not man who was first deceived. Moreover, woman will be saved only through child-bearing. Once again the appeal is to rabbinic exegesis of Genesis, on this occasion to Genesis 2.18–24 and 3.16, in order to support the author's plea for social order.[39]

Likewise the Titus and 1 Peter passages support my thesis: all arise from specific problems being experienced in the church and all tend to suppress the principle of 'equality' in favour of the expedient approach of cultural sensitivity and the maintenance of social order.

Conclusions

Two principles, then, govern the New Testament's interpretation of the relationship between man and woman. The first is equality in Christ and the creation of Man as male and female in the image of God (the restoration principle and first creation narrative). The second is submissiveness of woman to man, 'out of reverence for Christ' or 'as is fitting in the Lord', when social order and custom demand it (the priority principle in creation and fall as argued from the second creation narrative in Gen. 2.18–24 and Gen. 3.16). I have no hesitation in pronouncing the two positions contradictory in absolute terms but reconcilable on the basis of an ethic of love (which ethic I believe the Christian ethic to be).[40] It is also helpful to reflect on the injunctions to woman to be subordinate as *prescriptive*, attempting to re-establish patriarchal reality, rather than *descriptive*, as are the creation of man and woman in the image of God and the abolition of sex distinctions in Christ which affirm egalitarian reality.[41]

My hermeneutical approach is, I submit, a real option; I believe that it takes into account not only the radical nature of the gospel message and the cultural conditioning of the biblical text, but most importantly, the necessity at all times for cultural sensitivity and the maintenance of social order.

It remains to be said that the church must constantly seek to rediscover the nature of the radical gospel and apply it creatively and sensitively to the issues of the day. The radical gospel as lived by Christ and proclaimed by Paul affirms the equality and complementarity of the sexes. And so it seems to me that cultural sensitivity and the maintenance of social order in the climate which prevails in late twentieth century Western society clearly demands the unequivocal affirmation and implementation of this gospel truth.

4: Daughters of Eve
Women in Christian history

> I am Eve, the wife of noble Adam; it was I who
> violated Jesus in the past; it was I who robbed my
> children of heaven; it is I by right who should have
> been crucified.
>
> I had heaven at my command; evil the bad choice
> that shamed me; evil the punishment for my crime
> that has aged me; alas, my hand is not pure.
>
> It was I who plucked the apple; it went past the
> narrow of my gullet; as long as they live in daylight
> women will not cease from folly on account of that.
>
> There would be no ice in any place; there would be
> no bright windy winter; there would be no hell,
> there would be no grief, there would be no terror
> but for me.[1]
>
> Anonymous, Old Irish

Throughout the church's history, a majority of Christians have
seen Eve no longer as the blessed mother of all living but as the
mother of all sinners, temptress and seductress par excellence, the
epitome of feminine wiles and female weakness.[2] She is to be
paralleled and replaced by a new or Second Eve, Mary – ever
virgin, merciful and tender, the epitome of feminine virtue, in
early Christian, Catholic and Orthodox theology, and by the
Virtuous Wife – demure and obedient helpmate to her strong and
noble lord in the Reformed tradition.

The earliest Christian communities were fired with great zeal
and enthusiasm in worship and evangelism as they awaited the
return of Jesus Christ in glory, to usher in the kingdom. They
had good news to be shared by all, and the more people who told

it, the better, women as well as men. But before long, the church's genuine concern for order and cultural sensitivity in evangelism, and even more so its theologians' tendency to conform to the thought-patterns, philosophical systems and social structures of their surroundings ensured that throughout most of its history women have been treated as 'daughters of Eve' rather than as 'children of God' or 'sisters in Christ'. Already in the New Testament period we have noted the inclination to fall back on rabbinic exegesis of the creation narratives in order to support the status quo. And as the eschatological, other-worldly, hope of the imminent return of Jesus Christ faded, the church found itself under even greater pressure to set up structures to ensure survival in this world. A parallel need developed to move from a generalised evangelistic and teaching ministry by 'apostles, prophets and teachers' to a more localised ministry of 'bishops, priests and deacons'. We observe, therefore, early development from a charismatic Spirit-controlled ministry – where men and women alike were endowed by the Spirit with gifts for church planting, prophecy and teaching – to a structured, official ministry which conformed to the norms of patriarchal society and the Greek hierarchical order.

Charismatic ministries where women functioned freely as prophets and healers continued to exist on the 'heretical' fringes of the church in, for example, Gnosticism and Montanism.[3] And by and large as the church spread into Europe, its patriarchal structure and hierarchical order were reinforced by a similar Germanic world view. And yet, as we shall see, at particular periods of missionary expansion (when the young church throbbed with life, as for example in early North Africa, Anglo-Saxon England and sub-Saharan Africa today) and during revivals of religion (such as the Evangelical Revival in Britain and the Great Awakenings in America) charismatic ministries flourished. As new life came to all, men and women alike, barriers were broken down and sons and daughters prophesied. But, once again, order was before long called for and social context confirmed. A literal reading of Scripture and a respect for tradition dictated the form ministry would take.

There is one further ambivalence which we may discern about
the position of women in church and society. For whatever men
may write or say about women (opines Roland Bainton) they listen
to them, often yield to them, allow themselves to be governed by
them and at the same time give them little credit. And any psychologist or anthropologist would be glad to suggest any number of
reasons why.

1. Wives, prophets, widows and deacons: women in the early church

(i) Wives

When alluding to Paul's instructions to husbands and wives in 1
Corinthians 7 and in the household codes of Colossians 3 and
Ephesians 5, we made no comment on his views regarding the
married state. Paul states categorically (in his own opinion but not
by command of the Lord) that the widowed and the unmarried
should stay in their single state because of impending doom and
the end of the world (1 Cor. 7.8, 25–26). But if for reasons of
passion Christians cannot refrain from sexual activity then it is
better that they marry, each man having his own wife and each
woman her own husband. (Incidentally, it is not Paul but the
Corinthians who say, 'It is well for a man not to touch a woman',
1 Cor. 7.1). Nevertheless, Paul, when writing to the Corinthians
appears to view marriage and, therefore, the wifely calling as less
than the highest because it is tainted with sex. Yet, when writing
to the Ephesians, he exalts the marriage relationship to a great
'mystery': a wife must be subject to her husband as the church is
subject to Christ while a husband must love his wife as Christ
loves the church (Eph. 5.21–6.9). We discern, therefore, a certain
ambiguity, also apparent in the Pastoral Epistles, which in the
Fathers of the church was to develop into misogynism and the
exaltation of virginity. However, at the end of the New Testament
period, it is still generally true that a woman may somehow redeem
herself by being a good wife and mother: '[she] will be saved
through bearing children, if she continues in faith and love and
holiness, with modesty' (1 Tim. 2.15).

(ii) Prophets

As already mentioned there were women in the early church who were prophets. No distinction seems to be made between the office as exercised by men and women: they each speak the inspired word of God as occasion demands, with respect to special events (Acts 21.7–14) and in the public assembly of Christians (1 Cor. 14). Moreover, prophets come second in Paul's threefold charismatic ministry of 'apostles, prophets and teachers' (1 Cor. 12.28), often considered the earliest form of Christian ministry, replaced later by the more localised ministry of bishops, priests and deacons. Some writers associate prophecy with prayer and on this basis argue for a continuing role for women in the public prayers and liturgy of the church.[4]

(iii) Widows and Deacons

Already in the New Testament we discern the beginnings of what were to become two distinct offices for women in the early centuries of the church: the order of widows (1 Tim. 5.3–16) and the order of deacons (1 Tim. 3.11).[5]

Widows in the Pastoral Epistles feature as three different but not unrelated entities: 'aged widows' cared for by the community (Acts 6.1–2, 9.39); 'godly women' who train up the young wives to love their husbands and children (Titus 2.3–4); and 'real widows' who remain alone, set their hope on God and continue in supplications and prayers to God night and day (1 Tim. 5.3–10). The third category with its emphasis on the ascetic and contemplative calling anticipates what was to become an order of widows. In the literature they are variously associated with a ministry of prayer, the pastoral care and teaching of women in their homes, the care of the sick, instruction of women generally and charitable service.[6] Clement of Alexandria (c AD 155–220), Origen (AD 184–254) and Tertullian (African Church Father c AD 160–c 220) seem to number them among the clergy; as one of four orders they are listed with or without 'the laying-on-of-hands' (ordination) as belonging with the bishops, priests and deacons.[7] Tertullian specifically mentions them alongside the presbyters in the congregation;[8] as such they developed along independent lines in an oriental culture which required strict segregation of the sexes, necessitating the sending of women to minister in the women's quarters. Gradually, however, they began to be restricted in their functions: they were explicitly forbidden to baptize and excluded from ordination, as 'Ordination is for the clergy, because they perform the liturgical services, while the Widow is instituted for prayer, which is a function of all Christians.'[9] By the middle of the third century the order had entered into decline and by the end of the fourth it had disappeared altogether. Most likely its disappearance is to be associated with the development of the male diaconate and the growing strength of the presbyterate and monarchical episcopate. As the church grew and became institutionalised clear lines had to be drawn between 'orthodoxy' and 'heresy'. Women, it was felt, conscious of the large part which they played in the early expansion of the church, were likely to abuse their position and make impossible demands, often on the heretical fringe. Tertullian, for example, commenting on the 'heretical' Marcionite Church which claimed to be the successor of the Pauline communities rails against women:

> What effrontery we find amongst these female heretics! They actually dare to give the church's teaching, to engage in disputations, to practise exorcism, to promise cures, perhaps even to baptize!

And elsewhere he continues:

> Women are not permitted to speak in the church, but equally they are forbidden to give the official teaching, to baptize, to make the Offering or to lay claim to any function (*munus*) of men, or of the sacerdotal ministry (*officium*).[10]

Similarly, the Council of Laodicea, meeting in AD 343, declared that in future women might not be appointed elders (*presbyterae*) in the church.[11] It must not be forgotten that by this time the presbyters had in effect become cultic priests with sacramental functions considered inappropriate to women.

On the decline of the order of widows, which was to some extent autonomous and independent, another institution arose to take its place: the order of *deaconesses* or the female diaconate. It was intended to be a passive tool of the bishop, with a fixed place in the church's hierarchy. Deacons in the New Testament feature as ministers in certain parts of the church and are called upon to be 'serious, not double-tongued, not addicted to much wine, not greedy for gain' and to hold 'the mystery of the faith with a clear conscience' (1 Tim. 3.8–10). Similarly, female deacons were to be 'serious, no slanderers, but temperate, faithful in all things' (1 Tim. 3.11). Their calling was to serve. Origen used Phoebe's position as a deacon at Cenchreae (Rom. 16.1) to argue for women of like calibre to be admitted to the church's ministry.[12] Clement likewise appealed to Paul's 'directions about women deacons'.[13] The deaconesses took over some of the duties of the widows. In particular, they played a special role in anointing female candidates for baptism by immersion (for reasons of decency) and instructing them afterwards in the faith, and visiting and caring for Christian women who lived in heathen households. They were considered to parallel the deacons and so underwent a service of ordination in which, at least in some instances, they were vested with a stole and given a chalice.[14] Eventually, however, under ascetic influences and following the ideal of virginity, the order became absorbed into the monastic life of the cloisters. In monasticism the deaconess often became 'head deaconess' of a local community or convent or an 'abbess' and in the Eastern Church performed limited liturgical functions. In the Western Church the order did not appear until the fourth century and then mainly in an honorary form under Greek influence.[15]

It remains to note that the restrictions of age placed on both widows and deaconesses probably point to the exclusion of women from the sanctuary because of sexual taboos connected with menstruation and pregnancy. This was due partly to the revival of Old Testament regulations about purity in the late classical and early medieval periods, but no doubt also to the existence of such taboos in European cultures. The taboos remain to this day and, albeit subconsciously, continue to affect the place of women in the church.[16]

2. Whores, wives or virgins: women in patristic theology

(i) Eve the source of sin

In addition to its allusion to rabbinic exegesis of the fall as related in Genesis 3 (1 Cor. 11.7; 1 Tim. 2.9–15) the New Testament also contains overtones of Jewish apocalyptic and pseudepigraphical interpretations of the episode concerning the giants in Genesis 6, where 'the sons of God' take to wife 'the daughters of men' (Jude vv. 6–7, 14; 2 Pet. 2.4). In the literature the two stories begin to come together until the latter blends almost imperceptibly into the former. The serpent is identified with Satan and 'the sons of God' with the angels or heavenly beings. Satan envies Adam as the image of God and so sexually seduces Eve who in turn dupes Adam. The angels allow themselves to be enticed or even seduced by beautiful women and as a result fall into grievous sin. And for ever after women are to be associated with the cause of evil and the power of the sexual drive. Every woman has become an Eve, indicted as the cause of evil and the corruptor of men and angels. This is precisely the view taken over by the Fathers of the church, elaborated and interpreted in Greek philosophical terms and handed down to us in the form of Christian tradition.[17]

(ii) Sin and sexuality

Early Fathers such as Justin Martyr (c AD 100–165), Irenaeus of Lyons (c AD 130–c 200), Clement of Alexandria, Origen and Tertullian variously associate women with the seduction of the angels and the consequent wickedness of the human race, blame Eve for the entry not only of death but of concupiscence and lust into the world as the result of the first sin and try to exonerate Adam as a naïve innocent. But they maintain some balance, as, for example, when both Justin and Irenaeus depict Mary by her obedience bringing forth Christ to undo what the virgin Eve brought about by her transgression and, when Clement insists that the marriage act and generation were created by God and are therefore good.[18]

Two practical implications of these views are that woman should dress modestly because of her shame and have her children baptized because she has conceived and given birth in uncleanness.[19] Two quotations from Clement and Tertullian respectively give us a flavour of the times. Clement insists that except when at home women should be modestly covered:

> For that style of dress is grave, and protects from being gazed at. And she will never fall, who puts before her eyes modesty and her shawl; nor will she invite another to fall into sin by uncovering her face.[20]

Tertullian asserts that although the disobedience of Eve is offset by the obedience of Mary, women must nevertheless continue to bear the shame of the first sin and seek to expiate it:

> If there dwelt upon earth a faith as great as is the reward of faith which is expected in the heavens, no one of you at all, best beloved sisters, from the time that she had first 'known the lord,' and learned [the truth] concerning her own (that is, woman's) condition, would have desired too gladsome (not to say too ostentatious) a style of dress; so as not rather to go about in humble garb, and rather to affect meanness of appearance, walking about as Eve mourning and repentant, in order that by every garb of penitence she might the more fully expiate that which she derives from Eve, – the ignominy, I mean, of the first sin, and the odium [attaching to her as the cause] of human perdition. 'In pains and in anxieties dost thou bear [children], woman; and toward thine husband [is] thy inclination, and he lords it over thee.' And do you not know that you are [each] an Eve? The sentence of God on this sex of yours lives in this age: the guilt must of necessity live too. *You* are the devil's gateway: *you* are the unsealer of that [forbidden] tree: *you* are the first deserter of the divine law: *you* are she who persuaded him whom the devil was not valiant enough to attack. *You* destroyed so easily God's image, man. On account of *your* desert – that is, death – even the Son of God had to die.

And do you think about adorning yourself over and above your tunics of skins?[21]

In fairness to Tertullian it should perhaps be added that elsewhere he paints a charming picture of husband and wife sharing in their devotions.

The later Fathers, although not always so extensively or directly also rely on the same extra-biblical sources to inform their views of women. We shall look at three, Gregory of Nyssa (c AD 330–395), Augustine of Hippo (c AD 354–430) and Jerome (Bible translator, c AD 342–420), in order to discover how they constructed a theology of sexuality which was to have enormous implications not only for the church but also for the history of Western civilisation.[22]

In Greek thought (especially the Platonic and neo-Platonic) spiritual reality was one or unitary – monistic: duality only appeared with matter. Therefore, the being of God cannot be dual nor can the image of God in Man be bisexual: God is spirit and his image is a spiritual one. The consequence of this kind of thinking was to make the being of God and therefore his image in Man either male (thus rendering the female secondary) or nonsexual. Gregory of Nyssa chose the latter course and Augustine of Hippo (most influential) the former.

The outworking of Gregory's thought with regard to sexuality means that Man was created originally as a spiritual nonsexual being. But 'with a view to the fall' God added a bodily nature bisexual in character. The spiritual nature to which Man is restored in redemption does not, however, preserve this bisexuality because, like Christ, resurrected Man is 'neither male nor female' (Gal. 3.28). As to whether or not marriage exists in Paradise Gregory is undecided. Thus, for Gregory, the image of God in Man is spiritual and monistic and not material and dualistic. 'Bisexuality pertains to that lower nature which both drags man down to sin and death and provides a remedy in procreation, but redemption is return to the monistic nature of the angels.' The virgin or monk becomes the soul redeemed from the duality of bodiliness to return to the monism of the heavenly world. The result of all this is that although sex and marriage are not bad they are not necessarily good and certainly they are not the best means to Man's highest fulfilment.[23]

Augustine's major departure from Gregory is that he makes bisexuality more intrinsic to creation. But he does so by assimilating maleness into monism, so making femaleness rather than bisexuality its lower, bodily nature. Adam is a compound being, comprising both male spirituality and female bodiliness. When Eve is taken from Adam's side she symbolises the bodily side of Man, taken from him in order to be his helpmate, but only for the bodily task of procreation, for which she is indispensable. Augustine, admittedly but inexplicably, does affirm that Eve too has a rational nature, being likewise a compound of spirit and body. Yet, in relation to man she stands for body vis-à-vis male spirit. This is her 'nature'. Consequently, in Augustine, by nature as well as on account of sin woman is man's inferior, symbol of a debasing carnality which draws the male mind down from its heavenly heights:

> A good Christian is found in one and the same woman to love
> the creature of God, whom he desires to be transformed and
> renewed; but to hate the corruptible and mortal conjugal
> connection and sexual intercourse: *i.e.* to love in her what is
> characteristic of a human being, to hate what belongs to her as
> a wife.[24]

There is, however, another string to Augustine's bow. If Man as originally created before the fall was bisexual rather than nonsexual he was nevertheless nonsensual. Thus, Augustine finds an outlet for his aversion to passion and sensuality in sex. He locates sin in the male erection and therefore finds in woman its occasion and cause. The sexual relationship is thus deprived of all the qualities that make it personal. When a man performs the sex act, whether to satisfy his lust or to implant his seed, he is forcing the woman to allow him to use her as a sex object, as an instrument to an impersonal end. In no way can the relationship become an 'I-Thou' relationship of personal encounter. And this depersonal-

ised view of sexual relations gives the basic images of the possibili
ties for woman in the Fathers. As *whore* she entices man – the
rational male – to wallow in the flesh; as *wife* she surrenders her
body to her husband on command, deriving no personal pleasure
but allowing herself to be used solely as an instrument of procrea
tion; as *virgin* she rises to a spirituality and personhood equal to
the male, but only by denying her female nature and crushing her
body.

There is no space here to discuss in detail Augustine's view that
the sinful nature of the sex act, however good in intent, even
within marriage taints the resulting child with original sin.

Jerome takes the Augustinian view of original sin as transmitted
by sex to its final and logical conclusion. He seeks to persuade as
many Christians as possible to renounce marriage. He seems to
take every opportunity possible to write to women, usually of high
breeding, and pronounce against feminine wiles in order to extol
the ascetic ideal. Jerome's image of the spiritual woman is of one
who is an ascetic herself and also the 'mother of virgins', meaning
that she both encourages her own daughters to be virgins and
presides over a community of such. To one of these women he
writes:

> For you must act against nature or rather above nature if you
> are to forswear your natural function, to cut off your own root,
> to cull no fruit but that of virginity, to abjure the marriage-bed
> to shun intercourse with men, and while in the body to live as
> though out of it.[25]

Thus the defiling nature of sex and the image of the virginal
woman as ideal pass into Christian consciousness.

In Augustine's description of his mother, Monica, we are
provided with a picture of the Christian wife and in Jerome's
letter about his friend, Paula, an example of the virginal ideal.
Augustine, in his *Confessions*, describes his mother in glowing
terms as a Christian woman who served her husband 'as her lord',
bearing with patience his infidelity and bad temper until, towards
the end of his life, he was converted to God by her patient example.

For this she was greatly praised, honoured and loved by her fellow Christians.[26] Likewise, Jerome, in one of his many letters to women, praises to the point of extravagance his companion, 'the saintly' Paula, who helped him to build the monastic life in Palestine: she is an illustrious model of chastity and virginity. Leaving husband and children behind in order to pursue the spiritual life she spends her days mourning and fasting in squalor and weeping, the psalms her only songs, the gospel her whole speech.[27]

iii) Mary the new and Second Eve

The image of the virginal woman thus became a new cultural ideal, enabling women to attain the highest spiritual achievement – not, as once believed, by becoming male – but by communion with the divine intellectual nature of the deity.[28] Such heights had been previously reserved for men. Many streams of imagery flowed and converged to make up the portrait of the 'spiritual woman': the beloved of the Song of Songs, the bride of Christ and Sophia, the Wisdom of God. All these and more were gathered together by the end of the fourth century into Mariology. Mary is the Second Eve, epitome of all the images of spiritual womanhood. She is Queen of Heaven and Mother of God as was the Earth Goddess of the Mediterranean. But, concludes Rosemary Radford Ruether:

> Virginal woman was thus bound for heaven, and her male ascetic devotees would stop at nothing short of this prize for her. But they paid the price of despising all real physical women, sex and fecundity, and wholly etherealizing women into incorporeal phantasms in order to provide love objects for the sublimated libido and guard against turning back to any physical expression of love with the dangerous daughters of Eve.[29]

One cannot help but be reminded of Pope John Paul II's devotion to the Virgin and admiration for Mother Teresa of Calcutta who, in Indira Gandhi's opinion, radiates gentleness, love and compassion – feminine or ascetic virtues?

3. Equal souls and unequal sexes: women in medieval theology and piety

The medieval world mediates between the early Christian period and the modern. In it ancient classical, early Christian and Germanic world views merged to form a self-conscious Christian culture. It produced high theology and a rich and variegated popular piety which together provide us with a picture of woman reflected in popular assumptions to this day. It gave birth to extremes like the Albigensian sect which repudiated sex altogether and the practice of romantic and courtly love, the expression of which was usually extra-matrimonial. Towards the end of the period the position of woman was considerably weakened by the imposition of clerical celibacy during the Gregorian reform of the eleventh century. Throughout, the popular propaganda literature tended to disparage marriage and womanhood.

(i) A theological framework: Thomas Aquinas

Thomas Aquinas (c AD 1225–74), Dominican Doctor of the church modifies the predominantly Augustinian theology of his predecessors with insights gained from a naturalistic world view represented by Aristotelian philosophy and the natural sciences. In his discussion of creation Thomas, like Augustine, focusses on the Genesis 2 account. But by employing an Aristotelian anthropology he escapes from patristic dualism and bestows on Man a composite body and soul. Moreover, he gives the body a positive value by allowing it to achieve its own excellence through pursuing its own proper end. However, he does not manage to escape from a pessimistic evaluation of sex, because he follows the Fathers' rational definition of Man. Moreover, Man's chief end, life with God, is achieved by the operation of the rational soul. Ultimately therefore, the body is once again left out. Furthermore, following Aristotle, Thomas believes that the male is created for the more noble pursuit of intellectual activity, whereas the female, although possessing a rational soul, is created solely for the sexual bodily activity of reproducing and preserving the species. Similarly, following Aristotle, he maintains that the girl child represents a defective human being. No justification, other than reproduction, can be given for the existence of a 'second sex', because for any other activity – work or play – man would have been better served by a male helpmate. The subordination and inferiority of Eve – and therefore of all womanhood – is thus established before the fall: first by reason of Adam's primacy in time and as the material source of the woman; and second, because Adam displays the peculiar purpose and essence of human nature, intellectual activity, and Eve the auxiliary bodily, generative function. Yet, if there is inequality of the sexes there is a certain equivalence or equality of souls. For both sexes bear the image of God, with the ability to know and love him. That said, however, the male possesses the image to a greater degree than the female, because he demonstrates greater intellectual capacities; moreover, the female's weaker and less perfect body affects her intelligence, thereby impairing her moral judgment. The role of Eve in the fall serves only to worsen this natural subordination by bringing about male domination. Eve, as she falls, is not only proud, but weak, credulous and seductive, while Adam, although similarly proud, succumbs to temptation to attain the knowledge of good and evil and out of love for and solidarity with his spouse![30]

Only in the area of salvation from sin do we meet with a measure of equality between the sexes. Yet, even then, we encounter a male-centred christology: redemption can be achieved only through a male redeemer, a Second Adam, because the masculine sex is the more nearly perfect and strong. And, incidentally, it follows that only males can mediate the grace of Christ through the sacramental and teaching function of the priesthood. When Thomas, however, turns to discuss the redemptive role of Mary he partly redresses the balance because, as Eve 'began' the work of sin so Mary 'began' the work of redemption (although she is or does nothing apart from her Son). True and genuine equality of the sexes comes for Thomas only at the resurrection when male and female alike will share the beatific vision and love and enjoy God with perfect rationality.

(ii) Unequal sexes: marriage

Marriage was the least acceptable of the three options open to women: the virginal religious life, continent widowhood and 'if you must' marriage. But by the thirteenth century it had gained in importance, taking on the character of a sacrament which symbolised the indissolubility of the bond between Christ and his church and conveyed grace to a couple to fulfil the 'goods' of marriage. These goods were procreation, remedy for sin and sacrament.

The first 'good', procreation, served only to remind the woman of her subordination and auxiliary position in the marriage relationship for several reasons: she was but a passive receptacle in which the male sperm would grow; with defloration she lost her virginity; the education of her children was primarily the husband's responsibility because he was her 'head' biologically and morally.

The second 'good', remedy for sin, although theoretically allowing to each partner the right over the body of the other (1 Cor. 7.4) in practice made a greater number of exceptions for the man, as he had absolute control over his own body, a right which a woman did not have.

The third 'good', marriage as a sacrament, conferred grace which neutralised and legitimised conjugal sexuality; it also cemented indissolubility, a Christian innovation of great importance for the protection of the woman. Yet these benefits were somewhat nullified by the grounding of indissolubility primarily in the need to provide permanence for the children and only secondarily in the mutual well-being of the partners (protection from lust). One looks in vain in Thomas for the concept of sexual union as an outward sign, a sacrament, of marital love, fidelity and community. The notion of marriage as a physical relationship which can express or sustain a spiritual partnership for mutual growth and love has yet to come.

The popular didactic literature of the time addressed to wives and young girls emphasises that woman's domain is the house, that she should obey and honour her husband and that young girls should adapt their behaviour and attend to their appearance so as always to please the men.

(iii) Equal souls: the religious life

Both theoretically and practically, from the theological as well as the sociological standpoint, the virginal religious life offered to woman a means of escape from the natural subordination and inferiority of her sex. But it demanded a price, the denial of her essential womanhood and the devaluation of everything deemed to be feminine.

In the cloisters, woman could achieve the perfecting of her soul. But she did so only by assuming the nature of the male which was identified with true human rationality, strength, courage, steadfastness and loyalty, and by denying, through subjugation of the body, her nature as female which was identified with sexuality, weakness, dependence and credulousness.

In the cloisters, woman moved in her own domain. The hierarchy was a female one and she could develop gifts of leadership and organisation, using qualities of mind as well as body. But even then as she attended mass and had her confession heard by the priest, she was reminded of the natural dominance of the male – because she was excluded from exercising priestly functions.

In the early middle ages women played a large part in the history of monasticism, both East and West. Especially interesting is the role which they fulfilled in the early medieval institution of the double monastery. The origins of double monasteries are obscure but it is assumed that they were founded because the women were in need of men to work in the fields and administer the sacraments. In Anglo-Saxon England, where double monasteries were prevalent in the seventh and eighth centuries, the leader was frequently an abbess. These women were learned in the Scriptures; they taught; they administered great religious houses; and they evangelised alongside the men. When Boniface set out on his mission to Germany he was accompanied by six men and six women: the women like the men founded monasteries. And during the great monastic reform movement from the tenth until the twelfth century women flocked to follow the men into the new teaching, preaching and serving orders. But a male church could not cope, and by the time of the high middle ages the position of women in the monastic life had suffered a sharp decline.[31] They were bani-

shed inside the walls of convents where they followed the contemplative life, too dangerous to the male and too weak for the world.

One such contemplative and mystic, Mother Julian, a recluse
who lived in a cell adjoining the church of St Julian in Norwich,
has given to posterity the first book in English to be written by a
woman. Her *Revelations of Divine Love* were destined to become
a classic. The book is based on 'showings' or revelations which
came to her during a brief illness in 1373, when she was in her
thirtieth year. To peruse the pages is to breathe an air very
different from that of patristic and medieval theology, for Julian
dwells in the love of God and probes daringly and courageously
every available image to express her devotion to the Trinity. It is
Adam, interestingly enough, who falls, but he is loved from eter-
nity and in Christ falls into the womb of the Virgin. God, Jesus,
the Trinity are variously called Mother: '. . . God was rejoicing to
be our Father; rejoicing too to be our Mother'; 'For the almighty
truth of the Trinity is our Father: he makes us and preserves us
in himself; the deep wisdom of the Trinity is our Mother, in whom
we are enfolded'; 'Jesus Christ who sets good against evil is our
real Mother.'[32]

4. Good wives: women of the Reformation

The Reformation brought one fundamental change to woman: it
removed her from the cloisters and placed her firmly at the hearth.
This happened largely because Luther rejected medieval theology's
distinction between Christian life according to 'the precepts' and
according to 'the counsels of perfection'. The first, obedience to
the law of God, was binding on all Christians; the second, pursuit
of the virginal religious life, was required of a few. Luther would
have none of this. He could not countenance two classes of Christians: all alike are justified by grace through faith and God's
commandments are binding on every baptised Christian. The
outworking of this teaching and other ramifications of Reformation
emphases are to be seen in Luther's and Calvin's theology of
marriage and the beginnings of changes in the general status of

woman as she moved out of the cloisters into the proper spheres of a Christian's calling: the family and the world.[33]

(i) A new theology of marriage

Both Luther and Calvin affirm that marriage is ordained of God and therefore good: it is the natural and normal state or, as Luther goes so far as to say on occasion, 'a superior state'. Writing to three nuns in August 1524 on the grounds for abandoning monastic life and convent vows, Luther speaks of virginity as a gift bestowed by God only on one in several thousands, and continues:

> A woman does not have complete mastery over herself. God so created her body that she should be with a man and bear and raise children. The words of Gen., ch. 1, clearly state this, and the members of her body sufficiently show that God himself formed her for this purpose. Just as eating, drinking, waking, and sleeping are appointed by God to be natural, so God also wills that it be natural for a man and a woman to live together in matrimony. This is enough, therefore, and no woman need be ashamed of that for which God has created and fashioned her, and if she feels that she does not possess that high and rare gift, she may leave the convent and do that for which she is adapted by nature.[34]

In similar vein Calvin writes in his *Institutes of the Christian Religion* when commenting on the seventh commandment:

> Man has been created in this condition that he may not lead a solitary life, but may enjoy a helper joined to himself [cf. Gen. 2:18]; then by the curse of sin he has been still more subjected to this necessity. Therefore, the Lord sufficiently provided for us in this matter when he established marriage, the fellowship of which, begun on his authority, he also sanctified by his blessing. From this it is clear that any other union apart from marriage is accursed in his sight; and that the companionship of marriage has been ordained as a necessary remedy to keep us from plunging into unbridled lust.[35]

We detect in both these theologians and others of the Reformation a shift towards a positive statement about marriage as companionship: it is not only for the purposes of procreation and a remedy for sin (a cure for concubinage), nor solely a legal enactment but a spiritual covenant entered into by the partners' own consent and commitment. Thus the Christian household becomes in a new way the place where Christian character is formed, and the Christian family takes its place as an important instrument of God in society. The husband is head in the home, because both Luther and Calvin follow the household codes of the New Testament. However, Calvin specifically states that as wives are to submit to their husbands so all Christians are to be subject one to another, and a husband must not oppress his wife.

A similar shift from progeny to companionship as the primary end in marriage appears to have occurred among the Puritans in England.

(ii) A new status for woman

The Reformation did not make a conscious effort to change the status of women, except in so far as Luther railed against 'papists . . . and all who despise the female sex'. But the removal of woman from the cloisters to the home initiated changes which were to have far-reaching consequences. Yet, even then, any analysis must not forget to take into account the effects of the Renaissance and the re-emergence of contraceptive techniques in the eighteenth century (incidentally, a factor which must never be underestimated for its social effects).

Three areas allow for some comment: changes in *marriage law*; growth of *public education*; and developments in *church life*.

The Reformers in general no longer consider marriage a sacrament in the medieval sense but rather an ordinance of God and a mutual commitment of two persons. They proceed to have the marriage laws revised, often by the civil authorities. They lay more stress on parental consent and the right of individuals to choose their partners, and encourage public registration of marriages and the performance of matrimony within the framework of public worship. Most innovative is their introduction of divorce and remarriage of the injured party (although not freely) and also, as for example in the Geneva Marriage Ordinances of 1561, the right of a woman to divorce her husband for adultery.

Luther lays strong emphasis on the priesthood of all believers and the liberty of the individual Christian, and, as a consequence, on the desirability of making the Scriptures available to all. This perhaps accounts for his call for public education for boys and girls alike as early as 1524. Also, in Geneva after 1536 all children are required to attend school, girls and boys alike learning reading, writing, arithmetic and catechism. No doubt the learned, noble and cultured Renaissance women provided added impetus and example.

It is often remarked that with the disappearance of nuns in Protestantism there was lost to women one visible, official role in the church, never widely replaced. This is true only up to a point, as continental Protestants at the end of the sixteenth century revived the diaconate or order of deaconesses for the purposes of distributing alms and nursing; also a new breed of woman emerged, the pastor's wife, called by one writer the 'pilot model of the new woman'. Luther's wife, Katherine von Bora, and Katherine Zell, wife of the Strasbourg Reformer, provide us with two good examples of the type. Luther's wife helped him experience the goodness of marriage. With enormous skill she managed a large household of husband, children, students, relatives and refugees with little money in a large old monastery. And Luther writes of her with admiration and affection. Katherine Zell was of a more fiery nature with a self-made public career. She defended her husband's right to marry by pamphlet and address, quoting the apostle Paul and the prophet Joel in support of woman's right to speak and liking herself in turn to Balaam's ass (unpretentiously castigating his master) and Mary Magdalene announcing the resurrection. After the death of her two infants she devoted much time to caring for refugees and visiting the sick.

5. Prophesying daughters: women in revivals of religion

The Evangelical Revival in Britain and the Great Awakenings
in America together with their offshoot, the nineteenth-century
Missionary Movement, gave birth to another 'new kind of woman'
for the times: the preacher. She features variously as 'prophet',
'evangelist', 'missionary', 'class teacher' and 'preacher', eventually
in some denominations being admitted to the ordained ministry.

I am inclined to attribute this new role allotted to women to the
fresh vitality which accompanies all movements of revival and
renewal and frequently results in the widespread use of the charismatic gifts, including prophecy. But other not unrelated explana-
tions also fit the circumstances: an implicit egalitarianism; an
emphasis on Christian experience; and a certain pragmatism which
encourages experimentation with new cultural patterns.

(i) John Wesley and English Methodism

In Britain it is John Wesley who is often seen as the key innovator,
so much so that one social historian goes so far as to say that
'emancipation of womanhood began with John Wesley'.[37] Wesley's
teaching on sin and the priesthood of all believers operated as a
great leveller across all barriers of class and creed; his emphasis
on religious experience contributed to a weakening of traditional
religious authority as rich and poor, educated and uneducated,
men and women alike testified to the work of grace in their lives;
and his encouragement of new forms of ministry (for example,
field preaching and class meetings) allowed for validity to be judged
by results. And so as early as 1739 Wesley appointed women as
'class leaders' in Bristol, in 1787 welcomed one Sarah Mallet as a
preacher and, in giving approval to the preaching of Mary Bosan-
quet, wrote: 'I think the case rests here, in *your* having an extraordinary call. So I am persuaded has every one of our lay preachers;
otherwise I could not countenance his preaching at all.'[38] Thus the
way is paved for the Methodist Bible commentator, Adam Clarke,
in the early years of the next century, to say of women that 'under
the blessed spirit of Christianity, they have equal *rights*, equal

privileges, and equal *blessings*, and, let me add, they are equally
useful.'[39]

(ii) Charles Finney and American Revivalism

Across the Atlantic the Great Awakenings produced similar prac-
tices. Women preachers appeared, for example, in the last decades
of the eighteenth century among the Free-Will Baptists. But it was
especially the revivalism of Charles G. Finney, expressing the
values and ethos of the Wesleyan Revival – the same thrust towards
egalitarianism, enthusiasm and pragmatism – which was to bring
in its wake both the full ordination of women and the rise of
feminism.

The most controversial of the new measures introduced by
Finney into his meetings was permission for women to pray in
mixed assemblies. But when challenged he refused to back down.
Finney became the first professor of theology and second president
of Oberlin College, probably the first co-educational college in the
world. Oberlin was to make a major contribution to the women's
rights movements as it numbered many of its graduates among the
early feminists. They included Lucy Stone, who gained notoriety
for her egalitarian marriage and her refusal to change her name;
Antoinette Brown, the first woman to be fully ordained, a Congre-
gationalist; and Betsy Cowles, president of the second National
Women's Rights Convention.

It was, however, as also to a lesser extent in Britain, the
campaign against slavery which enabled evangelical openness to a
new role for women to be transformed into an active evangelical
feminism. Close connections are to be discerned between Finney's
revivalism, the anti-slavery movements and the women's rights
conventions. (The part played by the radical Quaker and Unitarian
connections is somewhat better known.) In the 1840's the
Wesleyan Methodists emerged as an abolitionist protest against the
Methodist accommodation to slavery. And it was the Wesleyan
Methodist pastor, Luther Lee, who at the ordination of Antoinette
Brown in 1853, preached the famous sermon on 'Women's Right
to Preach the Gospel'. In it he claims that the New Testament
refers to women as ministers and argues for the local character of

the Pauline prohibitions. In addition, the first Women's Rights Convention at Seneca Falls in 1848 was held in the Wesleyan chapel. Finally, the Wesleyans began to ordain women in the early 1860's.

But at least some of these convictions were shared by members of other denominations. Presbyterian/Congregationalist Jonathan Blanchard, the founding president of Wheaton College, was an ardent abolitionist who, in his *Debate on Slavery* with N. L. Rice, argued that 'the first alteration which Christianity made in the polity of Judaism was to abrogate this oppressive distinction of sexes' in which 'women had almost no rights; they were menials to their husbands and parents.'[40] Blanchard, like Luther Lee before him, preserved the teaching that 'the husband is the head of the wife' but not so B. T. Roberts, founder of the abolitionist Free Methodist Church and supporter of the ordination of women (in his *Ordaining Women*, 1891). Roberts urged the image of the business partnership, insisting that 'the greatest domestic happiness always exists when husband and wife live together on terms of equality.'[41]

(iii) The 'pentecostal' motif

When Baptist leader A. J. Gordon 'bred in the strictest sect of the abolitionists' argued for 'The Ministry of Women' in an 1894 article in the *Missionary Review of the World*, he used not the abolitionist egalitarian argument but rather one based on the 'dispensation of the Spirit' inaugurated at Pentecost when Joel's prophecy (quoted in Acts 2) that 'your sons and *your daughters shall prophesy*' finds fulfilment (italics mine). This same argument had been developed by evangelist Phoebe Palmer in a lengthy treatise entitled *The Promise of the Spirit* in 1859. Palmer was a prime mover behind the nineteenth-century 'holiness revival' under whose influence, during an evangelistic crusade in England, Catherine Booth, co-founder of the Salvation Army, it is claimed, first felt called to preach.[42] Many of the evangelical churches founded in the late nineteenth and early twentieth centuries in America explicitly endorsed and practised the ordination of women. Pentecostalism continued the focus on Pentecost and the

Holy Spirit which supports a role for women in the ministry in certain contexts. Since World War II, however, for a number of reasons (the increasing professionalism of the ministry for one) the practice has declined.

(iv) The philanthropic and missionary movements

Meanwhile in Britain both the Evangelical Revival and the Oxford Movement were having a similar if somewhat different impact on woman's position in the church.[43]

In 1865 William and Catherine Booth – on Catherine's insistence before their marriage – founded the Salvation Army along totally egalitarian lines, the army refusing 'to make any difference between men and women as to rank, authority and duties' and opening 'the highest positions to women as well as to men'.[44]

From 1857 bible women were being recruited and trained in the elements of nursing under the auspices of the British and Foreign Bible Society to distribute bibles among the poor.

The Church of England witnessed two distinctive movements on the women's front. In 1845, at Regent's Park in London, under the direction of Dr Edward Pusey, the first religious community for women in England since the Reformation was opened. By 1878 it was estimated that at least 700 women had adopted the religious life. In 1861, the Rev W. C. Pennefather founded, in partnership with his wife Catherine, a Female Missionary Training Home which later became the Mildmay Deaconess Institution. It was modelled after the continental Lutheran Kaiserswerth Institution founded in 1836 and, like Kaiserswerth, administered its own hospitals, dispensaries, rescue homes, orphanages and old peoples' homes. The deaconesses took responsibility also for night schools, clubs for boys and girls, district visiting and home nursing. The revival of the order of deaconesses in the Church of England soon followed in the years between 1862 and 1872.[45]

Thus by the mid-1860's in Britain there were at least four different patterns of women's ministry to be observed within the 'home' churches: the voluntary women engaged in pastoral and philanthropic visiting; the bible women and deaconesses of nonconformity and Pennefather; the newly established orders; and the deaconesses of institutional Anglicanism. In addition there was the recently founded Salvation Army. But at the same time the area of overseas missionary work remained largely a male preserve. It was conceded that wives could go abroad with their missionary husbands, and a few single women, often widows and daughters of missionaries, might be engaged to look after missionary children or to teach. There were also small numbers of women missionaries engaged in zenana educational work in India.[46] But in normal recruiting the traditional denominational societies turned women away. A woman's place was in the home and in any case women sent abroad were likely to get married with an unbecoming and wasteful haste. Moreover, the preaching of the gospel in any formal manner was in the main a clerical responsibility. The only likely role for a woman was supportive and philanthropic, for example in the teaching and nursing professions.

Yet, despite this, by the end of the century societies such as the Church Missionary Society, the China Inland Mission, the London Missionary Society and the Wesleyan Methodist Missionary Society were all employing women, and often on a fairly large scale. For example, up until 1887 the CMS did not formally recruit women – at most 9 per cent of its missionaries in the 1870's were women – but between 1891 and 1900, 388 women, or 56.46 per cent of its total intake, were women. The reasons for the change are to some extent debatable and uncertain, but there is no doubt that nonconformity, the revivalist and holiness traditions, the development of women's work 'at home' on the religious front, and the pressures of society, together with the determination of women themselves on the secular front, influenced CMS. After all, Hudson Taylor of the CIM, as early as 1868, had argued in favour of single women missionaries on the grounds that they would only be doing what was already accepted for women in church activities at home. And in 1895 he was to write: 'I think that women may do what God has given them the gift for, if they do it in a womanly way, and that what Paul wanted was order in the church and not talking, also that the husband should be the head.' Taylor was a pioneer. In the first party of eighteen missionaries who sailed under the banner of CIM in the *Lammermuir* in

1865 there were nine single women, two wives and seven men. In one of the last which converged on West China in 1949 there were thirty-eight women and only eleven men, ready for 'all manner of service', especially church building and church planting.[47]

Conclusions

With regard to women in the church's ministry we may generally conclude that: a pastoral ministry to women and the sick and aged has been open to women in every age; a sacramental ministry – save for emergency baptisms and in the exceptional case of abbesses who functioned as bishops in the middle ages – has been denied alike by catholics, orthodox and protestants; and the preaching ministry has been allowed only by radical movements or during periods of revival and reform. Similarly, with regard to woman's status in society, the general position is one of subordination to men with some exceptions during times of renewal and missionary expansion.

More specifically, I should like to suggest that a radical Christian egalitarianism is associated with revival, reform, missionary zeal and the related emphasis of religious experience and the priesthood of all believers. But as new spiritual movements settle down and become institutionalised, concern for social order, conformity to the norms of the surrounding patriarchal society and appeal to tradition ensure a return to inequality.

I am hopeful that the latter end of the twentieth century (which has already witnessed the ordination of women in parts of the Anglican Communion, mainstream Methodism and Presbyterianism) with its changing social order, new hermeneutic and ability to challenge tradition is heralding the time soon to come when the 'daughters of Eve', in accordance with gospel truth, will take their rightful place as children of God and sisters in Christ.

5: Sisters of Mary
The Women's Movements

Of the four Evangelists, Luke is the one who portrays Jesus as Saviour of the world, of all kinds and conditions of man: society's outcasts and oppressed, in particular the poor, the sick, foreigners and women. It is he who tells the story of Jesus in the house of Martha and her sister Mary at Bethany. Martha as mistress of the household is hostess and so busies herself 'serving', preparing a meal for her guest, while Mary sits at the Lord's feet listening to his teaching. However, Martha becomes distracted by all that has to be done and goes to Jesus and says, 'Lord, do you not care that my sister has left me to serve alone? Tell her then to help me.' But Jesus replies, 'Martha, Martha, you are anxious and troubled about many things; one thing is needful. Mary has chosen the good portion, which shall not be taken away from her' (Luke 10.38–42).

As a child I was always puzzled by this story. Why should the diligent and busy Martha be rebuked while the apparently idle Mary is commended? Later, when I consulted the commentators, I never felt satisfied that they had really grasped the point either. Patristic and medieval scholars used the passage to lend dominical authority to their preference for the contemplative to the active form of Christian life. Similarly, some modern expositors seemed to think that the story illustrated the relative value of two kinds of ministry, the liturgical and the diaconal. Recently, however, I believe that I have found the key.[1]

Mary is commended for taking her place at the feet of a rabbi to listen and learn to be a disciple. This was a place, as we have already observed, not allowed to Jewish women at the time. Martha is rebuked for allowing domestic duties to worry and distract her and is recommended to follow Mary's example. People – and that includes women, too – need to be fed with food for the soul as well as the body.

Thus Mary becomes for me a fitting symbol of emancipated and liberated womanhood. Already in the first century Jesus claims for Mary what the modern women's movements have striven so hard to achieve: ways and means for women to develop their full human potential as persons, endowed as well with gifts of mind and spirit as qualities of feminine beauty and homely usefulness.

1. Woman in Europe and America until the eighteenth century

The fortunes of woman in Europe waxed and waned from the early and late middle ages through feudalism, Renaissance and Reformation to the eighteenth-century Enlightenment.

In later Roman times a woman had equal authority with her husband over her children, some rights of inheritance, protection from divorce but no control over her dowry. As these laws came into contact with Germanic traditions they were modified and a wife came more under her husband's domination, although adultery was severely punished and, perhaps because women could become priests and prophetesses, she was often better educated. In feudal times her lot was ambiguous as she was the property not only of her husband but also of his lord. As heiress she could be married off with unseemly haste and, when annulment could be procured on grounds of relatedness, as often as seemed economically profitable. As wife of a tyrannical husband she sought extramarital love with her knightly and courtly lover. In France, as unmarried or widowed, she had all the rights of a man and ruled estates, administered justice, signed treaties and even played military roles as did Joan of Arc.

But in the sixteenth century laws were enacted which chained woman to the hearth, banishing her from 'masculine' positions and placing her more firmly under the guardianship of either her father, her husband or the convent. Prostitution continued to be one way of escape allowed by society. Evan an Augustine and a Thomas Aquinas could assert that the suppression of prostitution would bring about the disruption of society through debauchery.

It was generally recognised as the supreme type of vice serving as the greatest guarantee of virtue. Efforts of a Charlemagne and others after him failed to eliminate it.

In France, the single woman occupied a privileged position, but now only in theory as she did not have sufficient economic authority or social standing to exercise her rights and avail herself of her privileges. Two kinds of woman fared better – the sovereign and the saint, as Simone de Beauvoir so succinctly and engagingly puts it: 'Queens by divine right, and saints by their dazzling virtues were assured a social support that enabled them to act on an equality with men. From other women, in contrast, only a modest silence was called for.'[2]

Woman's legal status remained almost unchanged from the sixteenth century to the nineteenth, but among the privileged classes her lot improved. Renaissance woman, particularly in Italy, emerged strong and free: she was sovereign, civil and military leader, artist, writer and musician; she was also licentious and lawless. Sixteenth century woman applied herself to arts and letters and began to penetrate the world of men. And in the eighteenth century her freedom increased further, particularly among the rising middle classes. In England and France, as a result both of Reformation theology and Enlightenment science and philosophy, woman's lot in marriage began to improve. The idea of what has been called companionate marriage was developed. Marriage began to be seen as a contract between persons, the wife promising to love, honour and obey her husband and the husband in return promising to love, cherish and respect his wife. The wife thus remained in a subordinate position, but absolute patriarchy had been replaced by constitutional patriarchy. Moreover, if the wife was to be a fitting companion for her husband she must be educated, yet not so well as to be a threat to his position. The approach is well exemplified in Rousseau who at one level sees man and woman as equal human beings and at another as unequal sexually, a distinction which leads him to dedicate woman to husband and maternity by affirming that 'Women's entire education should be relative to men . . . woman was made to yield to man and to put up with his injustice.'[3]

Two things remain to be noted. Throughout the period, women of rank and wit, along with Erasmus and other men of learning, wrote in defence of woman, affirming her worth and demanding her real education. This, and woman's success, in turn called forth satire and ridicule from her detractors who revived all the old arguments from ancient and medieval times. From the early middle ages up until the Industrial Revolution a paradox held in relation to women: women of the lower and peasant classes, the common people, enjoyed, relatively speaking, more independence than their contemporaries among the nobility and upper classes. The former engaged in productive activity on the land and in commerce but were economically powerless; the latter held economic power but, confined to the home, were productively impotent. Save for exceptional cases – monarchs like Isabella of Spain, Catherine de Medici and Elizabeth of England, and saints like Catherine of Siena and Theresa of Avila – the same end ensued: woman's non-involvement in a world of men.[4]

In America, however, in the late seventeenth and eighteenth centuries woman's lot was considerably better than her European counterpart's. Along the frontier, in the contest between settlement and wilderness, American democracy was shaped. People became self-reliant, assured of their equality and resentful of class distinctions. A shortage of women and the wide range of female occupations which included the making of clothing, printing, the working of silver and even the management of farms, encouraged a rough equality. (This, perhaps, was to account for the lead given by America to the feminist cause.) By the end of the century, however, industrialisation and urbanisation were bringing in a new social hierarchy and increased sophistication, particularly along the Eastern seaboard. Education and professionalisation were growing apace, but for men only – even female midwives were being replaced by male physicians. Thus the frontier ideal of woman's partnership with man in many spheres of life gradually gave way to the 'cult of true womanhood', in which the 'true middle-class woman was depicted as pious, delicate, submissive, domesticated and pure.'[5]

2. The origins of feminism

Feminism's overriding concern is the conviction that woman is equal with man. This is not to say, however, as many detractors would suggest, that man and woman do not possess distinguishing characteristics. Rather, it means that, in terms of worth, women are equal with men because they share a common humanity as free and responsible persons. Feminism as a historical phenomenon, as a self-conscious protest movement, arose when men and women began to feel that woman had been consistently denied her rights of equality, thereby suffering injustice at the hands of man.[6]

(i) Two waves of feminism

There have been two waves of feminism or two women's movements, with an intermission. The first, from the 1840's–1920's, gathered momentum in the years of evolutionary optimism preceding World War I. The second, following the Depression of the thirties, World War II and the fifties' 'Baby Boom', began in the optimistic sixties, when everything seemed possible for space-age technological man, and is still with us – if just about – in the recessionary eighties. In the main, we shall be looking at the two movements in Britain and the United States of America, but will take a cursory glance elsewhere, particularly at France.

(ii) Three currents of thought

The rise of feminism in the late eighteenth and nineteenth centuries owes its origins to three intellectual traditions or currents of thought: (a) the egalitarian individualist tradition of the Enlightenment; (b) the evangelical revivalist tradition of the Evangelical Revival and the Great Awakenings; and (c) the socialist tradition of the English and French co-operative and communitarian movements and Marxism; or, as one writer succinctly puts it, to reason, religion and revolution.

It was also preceded in seventeenth-century revolutionary England by the conscious aspirations to equality of a number of middle-class women. In the midst of the immense social change

nvolved in the disappearance of feudalism and the birth of capita-
ism, when men were claiming for themselves freedom and equa-
ity, these women found themselves left out and began to ask why.
One Mary Astell, writing on marriage in the year 1700, asked: /

> If Absolute Sovereignty be not necessary in a State how comes
> it to be so in a Family? or if in a Family why not in a State;
> since no reason can be alleg'd for the one that will not hold
> more strongly for the other. . . .

nd again:

> If *all Men are born free*, how is it that all Women are born slaves?
> As they must be if the being subjected to the *inconstant,*
> *uncertain, unknown, arbitrary Will* of Men, be the perfect
> Condition of Slavery?[7]

And in arguing for the values of the new revolutionary society
against the old tyranny, these women perceived themselves as one
ocial group – half the human race – oppressed by another social
group – men – and saw the world as thereby deprived of woman's
distinctive contribution. Thus it can be said that they initiated
political feminism, feminism as a power struggle between two
ocial groups (to be strongly revived by twentieth-century radical
feminism). Of interest for our purposes is the way in which they
lealt with the arguments of two respected authorities: Aristotle
nd the Bible. If woman is 'defective' man it is not because of any
physical difference between the minds of the two but because of
he lack of educational and social opportunities for improving the
mind of woman. And if Adam's being formed before Eve proves
ier natural subjection to him then Mankind's being formed after
he animals proves his subjection to them. How absurd. As for
Paul, he is to be interpreted allegorically.[8]

a) *Reason: the egalitarian tradition.* The eighteenth-century
Enlightenment emphasised reason, natural law and the equality of
he rights of man. Its arguments inspired the French Revolution

which, although it did little to further the emancipation of women
in France, affected the cause of women's rights in England and
the United States of America. Mary Wollstonecraft, whose *Vindication of the Rights of Woman*, published in 1792, is an early feminist
classic and the recognised starting point of the women's movement
in Britain, had in 1790 published *A Vindication of the Rights of
Man* during a debate on the French Revolution and in 1792 crossed
the Channel to see the Revolution close at hand. The Enlightenment tradition as evidenced in Wollstonecraft can be explored and
elucidated through some of the concepts of the English empiricist
philosopher, John Locke (1632–1704). In Locke's view, every
individual has a basic right to freedom. This freedom is given
according to the law of nature and is independent of social relations. With it, however, goes the duty not to impinge on the
freedom of others, thus ensuring that all men are equally free. As
well as being God's law, the law of nature is a law of reason,
accessible to man by virtue of his being a rational being. Thus
every mature individual is capable of becoming independent and
autonomous in a natural society of other such individuals.
However, natural society does not always develop along
harmonious lines, as a consequence necessitating political society
which depends on common consent. Perhaps Locke's views on
marriage arise because he sees the family as political society writ
small: in opposing the patriarchal concept of political government
he must oppose the absolute rule of the husband in marriage.
Marriage becomes a contract between independent persons and
husband and wife as equal partners exercise joint parental authority
over their children. The implications of all this for woman is that
as an independent personality she has the right to do with her life
what she likes, within the constraints of the law of nature.

Wollstonecraft's argument, following this egalitarian individualist tradition, is to affirm that woman, like man, is a rational being
– it is reason which distinguishes Man from the animals – and is
primarily a human being rather than a sexual being. As a human
being, then, woman is a person before she is a female, as a man
is a person before he is a male. And human virtue is one and the
same for man and woman. If woman cannot fairly be judged to

possess the same virtues and duties as man, it is because she has not been given the freedom and equality of opportunity to develop her talents. For this she needs equal civil rights which will entail first of all removing one person's dependence on another, whether due to rank and privilege or extremes of wealth and poverty. Then will follow education which will enable a woman to be a wife and a mother of superior quality, and to enter professions such as medicine and midwifery or to engage in trading, commerce or farming.

In an appeal to 'reasonable man' to consider the importance of her remarks, Wollstonecraft makes it quite clear that uppermost in her mind is the emancipation of a companion to be 'a *helpmeet*' for man: 'a more observant daughter, a more affectionate sister, a more faithful wife, a more reasonable mother – a better citizen.'[9]

But more influential even than the *Vindication* was to be *The Subjection of Women* by the philosopher and politician, John Stuart Mill (1806–73), first published in 1869. Mill's concern was to show that 'the principle which regulates the existing social relations between the two sexes – the legal subordination of one sex to the other – is wrong in itself, and now one of the chief hindrances to human improvement; and that it ought to be replaced by a principle of perfect equality, admitting no power or privilege on the one side, nor disability on the other.'[10] This he does by holding that woman's traditional position has been determined by feeling not reason. This feeling is based on the general practice during the history of mankind which is in turn determined by the law of the strongest. Consequently, woman's subordination is a form of slavery, admittedly grown milder with time, but still nonetheless indicating subjection on the one side and privilege on the other. The modern world, however, is distinguished by the fact that human beings are born not to a 'station' in life but to freedom to utilise their faculties and improve their lot. The freedom of individual choice thus becomes the great new principle producing the best consequences for society as a whole. Yet, being born to a particular place rather than to freedom continues to be woman's fate. In this way, by proceeding from a statement of general social equality, Mill argues for the equality of woman. Furthermore, like

Wollstonecraft before him, he believes that woman's present nature reflects the system and woman's nature under a different system remains to be seen. But until it can be demonstrated that to give a woman freedom to direct her own life must needs prevent her from fulfilling her traditional role as wife and mother, it must be presumed otherwise. The more likely result – feared by her oppressors – is that she will become a marriage partner on equal terms!

Of special interest for our purposes is Mill's answer to the rejoinder that religion imposes a duty on a wife to obey to her husband:

> The Church, it is very true, enjoins it in her formularies, but it would be difficult to derive any such injunction from Christianity. We are told that St. Paul said, 'Wives, obey your husbands:' but he also said, 'Slaves, obey your masters.' It was not St. Paul's business, nor was it consistent with his object, the propagation of Christianity, to incite any one to rebellion against existing laws. The apostle's acceptance of all social institutions as he found them, is no more to be construed as a disapproval of attempts to improve them at the proper time, than his declaration, 'The powers that be are ordained of God,' gives his sanction to military despotism, and to that alone, as the Christian form of political government, or commands passive obedience to it.[11]

(b) *Religion: the evangelical tradition.* Like egalitarianism, evangelicalism embraced the Enlightenment emphases on natural law, equality and freedom with the frequently concomitant belief in the perfectibility of man and the coming of a new society, utopia or millennium. John Wesley in Britain and Charles Finney in America variously proclaimed sin as the great leveller, Christ as the Saviour of all kinds and classes and the Holy Spirit as the sanctifier or perfecter of the new person and harbinger of a new age. As we have already noted, for many people these teachings led to the declaration of woman's equality with man at every level. Acceptance of the doctrine of the priesthood of all believers emphasised equal access to God by all – man and woman, rich and poor, clergy and laity; belief in the bestowal of the Holy Spirit on every individual believer without distinction laid new stress on individual religion; and recognition of the gift of prophecy as being for 'sons and daughters' alike opened up the way for women as well as men to pray and speak in public and to preach.

The implications for the rise and growth of feminism were enormous and cannot be overestimated. Evangelicals, men and women alike, threw themselves wholeheartedly into fighting for the great causes of the day: the abolition of slavery, chastity, temperance, education and suffrage. Yet, evangelical preachers like Phoebe Palmer in America and Catherine Booth in Britain are often judged to fall short of feminism because they espoused the Scriptural injunction that a wife should obey her husband.[12] To my mind, and as I hope to demonstrate, the judgment is inadequate.

Phoebe Palmer was a Methodist lay evangelist from New York City who in her time founded the Five Points Mission, was involved in the founding of Garrett Biblical Institute and Drew Seminary, served as editor of the *Guide to Holiness*, and claimed some 25,000 converts in the course of her evangelistic campaigns in the United States, Canada and the British Isles. She shied away, however, from controversy and social issues such as abolitionism, concentrating instead on developing the experientially-inclined quest for holiness' movement. Yet, perhaps because of a need to defend her own role as evangelist and religious teacher, she emphasised some of the themes of abolitionism, albeit with a distinctive pentecostal theological slant. This may be seen in her important and influential treatise, *The Promise of the Father*, with which she concludes in prayer:

The Church in many ways is a sort of potter's field,
where the gifts of woman, as so many strangers, are
buried. How long, O Lord, how long before man shall
roll away the stone that we may see a resurrection.[13]

Her ministry and her writings influenced in turn Catherine Booth and Frances Willard. The latter is widely renowned through her

work as founder and long-time president of the World's Women's
Christian Temperance Union and author of *Woman in the Pulpit*,
a work which dealt not only with the ministry of women but more
subtly with issues like sexist language in the pulpit. Willard's
linking of the suffrage issue to the more widely supported temperance and prohibition causes probably played a major role in eventually winning the vote for women. Indeed, evangelicals in
America played a much more important role in influencing feminist
principles than their counterparts in Britain.

Catherine Mumford Booth is recognised by her son-in-law bio-
grapher as one who 'was to the end of her days an unfailing,
unflinching, uncompromising champion of woman's rights.'[14]

When only twenty-one, in 1850, Catherine challenged her local
Congregational minister, whom she greatly admired, because she
felt that he had said something which she considered derogatory
to woman as a moral being. After the usual courtesies she wrote:

In your discourse on Sunday morning . . . your remarks
appeared to imply the doctrine of woman's intellectual and
even moral inferiority to man. . . . Permit me, my dear sir, to
ask whether you have ever made the subject of woman's
equality as a *being*, the matter of calm investigation and
thought? . . . So far as Scriptural evidence is concerned, did I
but possess the ability to do justice to the subject, I dare take
my stand on *it* against the world in defending her perfect
equality. . . .
The day is only just dawning with reference to female education,
and therefore any verdict on woman as an intellectual being
must be premature and unsatisfactory. . . . I cannot believe that
you consider woman *morally* more remote from God than man
or less capable of loving Him ardently and serving Him
faithfully? . . .
  Experience also on this point, I think, affords conclusive
evidence. Who, since the personal manifestation and
crucifixion of our Lord, have ever been His most numerous and
faithful followers? On whom has the horrible persecution of

past ages fallen with most virulence, if not on the sensitive heart of woman? . . .

On the subject of the relation between husband and wife and the confusion, as she sees it, between 'subjection' and 'inferiority' Catherine goes on to declare that woman is subject 'not as a being' but only to her own husband. Even then, 'under the glorious provisions of Christianity', she maintains that things can be different:

The glorious provisions of Christianity come to those who are united in Christ . . . the wife may realize as blissful and perfect a oneness with her husband as though it [the curse] had never been pronounced. For while the semblance of it remains, Jesus has beautifully extracted the sting by making love the law of marriage and by restoring the institution itself to its original sanctity. . . . Oh, that men of noble soul and able intellect would investigate it [the subject of woman], and then ask themselves and their compeers, *why* the influence of woman should be so underestimated. . . . If it be only *partially* true that those who rock the cradle rule the world, how much greater is the influence wielded over the mind of future ages by the *mothers* of the next generation than by all the young men living!

In similar vein she writes to her future husband, William, in January 1853:

I believe two united in Him may realize as complete and blissful a union, morally and spiritually, as though the curse had never been pronounced. Else He has left incomplete the work of restoration. Till this true idea of marriage is better understood there will be few happy unions, few well-regulated families. Till the position and mission of woman is properly estimated and cared for, in vain shall we look for perfect *oneness* in parents, and real worth in children. The general system of female education is calculated to render woman anything but a helpmate to man and a judicious self-dependent trainer of children. How

JOHN ... S
UNIVERSITY
LIBRARY

can it be expected that a being trained in absolute subjection to
the will of another, and taught to consider that subjection her
glory, as well as an imbecile dependence on the judgment of
others, should at once be able to throw off the trammels of
prejudice and training, and assume that self-respect, self-reliance
and sound judgment which are indispensable to the proper
discharge of maternal duties? It is altogether unphilosophical to
expect such a thing. It would be a phenomenon in the history
of mind without a parallel. . . .

Never till she is valued and *educated* as man's equal will unions
be perfect, and their consequences blissful. One of the happiest
omens for English homes and England's future glory – moral
glory – is the light and enquiry spreading on this subject . . .
I intend to make myself acquainted with those natural laws on
the observance of which God has made health and happiness
so much to depend, more fully than I am at present. . . .

When Phoebe Palmer and her husband visited Britain in 1859
Catherine was keenly interested. She had read Mrs Palmer's books
and knew her as 'the principal figure in the meetings'; she was,
however, unable to attend any of the meetings because of ill health.
Yet she put her pen to good use in Mrs Palmer's defence. The
Rev Arthur Rees, a minister in Sunderland, had twice attacked
Mrs Palmer from the pulpit and subsequently published the attack
in a pamphlet. Catherine could not hold her peace and in response
issued her famous pamphlet entitled *Female Ministry*:

Making allowance for the novelty of the thing we cannot discover
anything either unnatural or immodest in a Christian woman,
becomingly attired, appearing on a platform or in a pulpit. By
nature she seems fitted to grace either. God has given to woman
a graceful form and attitude, winning manners, persuasive
speech, and above all, a finely-toned emotional nature, all of
which appear to us eminently *natural* qualifications for public
speaking.

As previously, she goes on to attack the lack of 'mental culture

he trammels of custom, the face of prejudice and the one-sided
nterpretation of Scripture' as 'handicaps' and then delights to ask
ather impishly:

> Why should woman be confined exclusively to the kitchen and
> the distaff, any more than man to the field and workshop? Did
> not God, and has not nature, assigned to man *his* sphere of
> labour, 'to till the ground and to dress it'? And, if exemption
> from this kind of toil is claimed for a portion of the male sex,
> on the ground of their possessing ability for intellectual and
> moral pursuits, we must be allowed to claim the same privilege
> for woman! Nor can we see the exception more *unnatural* in
> the one case than in the other, or why God in this solitary
> instance has endowed a being with powers which He never
> intended her to employ.

And in commenting on the supposed Scriptural prohibitions she
ffirms with unusual insight for her time:

> When the true light shines and God's words take the place of
> man's traditions, the Doctor or Divinity who shall teach that
> Paul commands woman to be silent when God's Spirit urges her
> to speak, will be regarded much the same as we should regard
> an astronomer who should teach us that the sun is the earth's
> satellite.[15]

Catherine Booth's was an evangelicalism which preceded
wentieth-century fundamentalism, and it is my guess that she
vould be horrified to find that literalistic and out-moded interpret-
tions of the Scriptures are being employed even in the 1980's to
onfine woman to her 'proper' place in the home.

Phoebe Palmer and, more especially, Catherine Booth expressed
he same convictions as Mary Wollstonecraft before them: the
atural right of woman to education in preparation for more inde-
endent living and better motherhood, and the right of a woman
o pursue a calling other than housework. Yet few evangelicals,
nore particularly in Britain, were to get involved in organised

feminism as such, perhaps because of their accepting, in accordance with their view of Scripture, the headship of man over
woman.

(c) Revolution: the socialist tradition. From the beginning, socialist
thinkers were for the most part also feminists. In the egalitarian
and evangelical traditions, individualism, with its emphasis on
personality and property, tended to lead to support of the traditional family. However, under socialism there is to be no private
property to pass on from one family or generation to the next, so
there will be no need to rear children privately and consequently
no need to tie woman to the home. Feminist thinkers influenced
by socialism are therefore much more likely to identify with radical
feminism and the elimination of monogamous marriage and the
nuclear family than are feminist thinkers influenced by
individualism.

The early nineteenth-century socialists were united by a conviction that a new social order in which individuals were allowed and
encouraged to compete with each other for access to resources
and in which they were restricted only by the negative freedom
of personal and property rights, was bound to lead to increasing
and recurrent economic crises on a large scale. They were agreed
also that such an order must be replaced by a system of production
and exchange which would do away with poverty and exploitation
through a redistribution of resources on the basis of the equality
of persons. They differed greatly, however, as to the means by
which to achieve these objectives. As the means differed so, too,
did the precise position of women in the new order. Some of the
more individualistic of the socialists such as Proudhon (French
1809–65) were notably anti-feminist.

William Thompson (c 1785–1833) was a follower of the Scottish
social reformer and pioneer of the co-operative movement, Robert
Owen (1771–1858). Thompson employs both individualist and
socialist arguments to claim equal rights for woman. An individual
must be allowed to regulate her own life for herself: equality of
rights is a necessary condition of such independence. Moreover,
perfect equality is attainable only in the future co-operative society

n which women will free themselves from their past domestic
lavery. Since all possessions and means of enjoyment will be
he property of all, they will be able to liberate themselves from
lependence on their husbands. Women as well as men will be
upported by the whole wealth of the community and women like
nen will contribute equally to the common good. Moreover, the
o-operative association as a whole will be responsible for the
ducation and support of the children, although (ambiguously)
vomen will continue to be responsible for the rearing of children.[16]

The French theorist, Charles Fourier (1772–1837), expresses
imilar views (although without the individualist reasoning of
Thompson). He bases them instead on his beliefs in happiness
hrough the maximisation of gratified desire or passions in co-
perative living. Workers will engage in a variety of different
rades and professions but the community will not be organised
n families because Fourier regards monogamous marriage and the
amily as inefficient both economically and in terms of a life of
ratified desire. The progress of a society is to be judged by
ts improvement of the status and position of women. Women's
beration becomes complete with the abolition of monogamous
narriage and the family. Children will be brought up collectively
y special work groups whose interests lie in this direction: 'Liber-
ted from the family and educated like men for the full develop-
nent of their faculties in attractive work and in love, women will
eveal their true capacities in surpassing men.'[17]

Karl Marx's (1818–83) distinctive contribution to socialist theory
es in his definition of man or the individual as a social being and
he related doctrine of class struggle. This enables him to bypass
ome of the problems encountered by individualist and earlier
ocialist political theorists, as they tried to resolve the conflict
etween the interests of the individual and society. Marx does not
ay any great attention to the woman issue: the liberation of
voman will come with the revolution. However, his emphases on
he class struggle and revolution have put Marxian socialists in the
ontinuing dilemma of subordinating the interests of women to
he greater goal of liberating the masses.

It is Marx's collaborator and friend, Friedrich Engels (1820–95),

who addresses more directly the subject of woman's equality with
man. According to Engels, the subordination of woman in and
through the family, together with the subordination of a slave
class, first arose as a result of the emergence of private property
and both will disappear with its eradication. With the transfer of
the means of production to common ownership, the single family
will cease to be the basic economic unit of society. Thus, private
housekeeping is transformed into a social industry and the rearing
and education of children becomes a communal responsibility.
However, it is the family and not marriage which will disappear.
Marriage will improve as equality leads to reciprocal love and
divorce becomes readily available to all.[18]

(iii) Two faces of feminism

Inherent in the traditions which we have briefly surveyed lie
contradictory principles which give rise to several different faces
of feminism. Two in particular interest us.[19] As a result of the
Reformation and the Industrial Revolution life was divided into
the two separate spheres of home and work and woman was bani-
shed to the home. Home thus became a place to live, but not to
work – the realm of wifeliness and motherhood.

On the one hand, egalitarian and evangelical feminists saw
woman's liberation as educating and freeing her to be a more
companionable wife and competent mother. Environment was believed to have played the major if not the sole part in making
woman what she had been heretofore. Therefore, to discover 'true
womanhood' and 'superior motherhood' the environment had to
be changed. But this was still to admit a difference of nature
between male and female. Thus began the myth of the 'feminine
mystique' or the cult of 'true femininity', later supplemented by
arguments from biology.

On the other hand, the socialist tradition hoped that the change
of the social order would get rid of the traditional family with its
roots in individualism and property-owning capitalism and would
free woman for work alongside man in the world. Child care and
children's education at the same time would be a communal

esponsibility. Any innate difference between male and female was thus minimised and blurred.

Even today, these two faces characterise respectively 'equal rights' and 'radical' feminism. To put the contradiction another way: conflict exists between what is seen as a woman's reproductive role in the family and her productive role in society. Evangelicals confuse the issues when they pit the interests of feminism against the interests of the family. As we shall see, the two are by no means incompatible.

. The first wave: equal rights and moral reform, 1840's–1920's

i) The issues

The distinctively feminist issues which arose at this time (and are still with us to some extent) were equality of educational opportunity, equality before the law and equal pay.

In France immediately after the Revolution there was some feminist agitation. Olympe de Gouges proposed a 'Declaration of the Rights of Woman' equivalent to the 'Declaration of the Rights of Man' in which she asked for the abolition of all male privilege. Before long, however, she went to the scaffold. The revolutionary women's clubs were closed in 1793 to be followed by the legalisation of female inferiority in the Civil Law Code promulgated by Napoleon I, who is reported to have once remarked, 'What we ask of education is not that girls should think, but that they should believe.' According to this code the husband had full legal powers over his wife, her property and her children, powers which extended through relatives even beyond the grave. The wife was legally obliged to obey her husband, and could not engage in legal transactions without his approval – which left her a legal minor. If the wife committed adultery, she could be imprisoned for two years and divorced, and if she was caught in the act and killed by her husband, he could not be charged with murder. A husband, however, could commit adultery with impunity. Only if he introduced a permanent mistress into the household could he be sued for divorce by his wife, and even in these circumstances she had no legal protection if she committed an act of violence against him. Further legal restrictions forbade women to attend public meetings, wear trousers and go out unchaperoned.[20]

In America, the Women's Rights Convention held at Seneca Falls in 1848 made a significant addition to the United States Declaration of Rights:

> We hold these truths to be self-evident: that all men and women are created equal; that they are endowed by their Creator with certain inalienable rights; that among these are life, liberty and the pursuit of happiness: that to secure these rights governments are instituted, deriving their just powers from the consent of the governed. . . .

and proceeded to an enumeration of those rights hitherto denied to women:

> The history of mankind is a history of repeated injuries and usurpations on the part of man toward woman, having in direct object the establishment of an absolute tyranny over her. To prove this, let facts be submitted to a candid world. He has never permitted her to exercise her inalienable right to the elective franchise.
>
> He has compelled her to submit to laws in the formation of which she had no voice . . . .
>
> He has made her, if married, in the eye of the law, civilly dead.
>
> He has taken from her all right in property, even to the wages she earns.
>
> He has made her, morally, an irresponsible being, as she can commit many crimes with impunity, provided they be done in the presence of her husband.
>
> In the covenant of marriage she is compelled to promise obedience to her husband, he becoming to all intents and purposes, her master.
>
> He has so formed the laws of divorce as to what shall be the proper causes, and in case of separation, to whom the

guardianship of the children shall be given, as to be wholly regardless of the happiness of women. . . .

He has monopolized all the profitable employments, and from those she is permitted to follow, she receives but a scanty remuneration. He closes against her all the avenues to wealth and distinction which he considers most honourable to himself.

He has denied her the facilities for obtaining a thorough education, all colleges being closed against her.

He allows her in church, as well as state, but a subordinate position. . . .

He has created a false public sentiment by giving to the world a different code of morals for men and women. . . .

He has endeavoured, in every way that he could, to destroy her confidence in her own powers, to lessen her self-respect, and to make her willing to lead a dependent and abject life.[21]

In Britain, in 1856, the 'Ladies of Langham Place', a group of radical dissenters including Quakers and Unitarians, organised themselves into a committee to collect petitions for a Married Women's Property Bill and in 1858 founded the *Englishwoman's Journal* to air the issues. In 1859, a Society for Promoting the Employment of Women was founded. Later, Emily Davies, leader of the campaign to open up higher education to girls, and Elizabeth Garrett Anderson, the first woman doctor, were both drawn into the circle. Moreover, it was this same group of women who started the suffrage campaign in the 1860's.

The initial aim of the Langham Place circle was to reform the legal position of married women in respect to infant custody, divorce, property and earnings.

Thus, the battle for legal rights or equality before the law was an important aspect of the early feminist movement in Britain, America and France. This was in part due to the fact that the law was unable to protect the interests of women left defenceless by the doctrine of the unity of married couples. Without a legal identity of her own, a deserted or ill-treated wife was unable to use the law to defend her interests. Moreoever, as we have seen, within marriage she had no rights over her own person, her own property (for even if protected by trust she was denied the use of it), her earnings and even her own children.

But even more important was the struggle to enlarge employment opportunities and, as a necessary prerequisite to this, to improve the educational qualifications of those seeking employment. Secondary and higher education for girls became the aim.

Later, the demand for an end to the double standard of sexual morality, temperance and the abolition of slavery were to become dominant and, as a means to achieving this social and moral reform, votes for women.

(ii) The achievements

The battle was long and fierce and, indeed, is not yet over. It is easy, however, for us to forget that it is not yet forty years since women were first admitted to degrees at Cambridge University and gained the vote in France, while as recently as 1982 Americans failed to ratify the Equal Rights Amendment.

Following the setbacks after the Revolution in France organised feminism did not re-appear until 1870, apart from a few protests between 1848–51. The Roman Catholic Church supported the Napoleonic Code, opposing divorce, for example, by insisting that 'women belong to the family, and not to political society, and nature has made them for domestic cares, and not for public functions', and similarly withstanding the secularisation of education. Not surprisingly, therefore, feminism in France was anti-clericalist and moderate feminism Protestant-led, facts which at first helped but later hindered the cause.

In April 1870, Léon Richier and Maria Deraismes founded the Society for the Improvement of Women's Lot to demand the reform of the Napoleonic Code. Adopting a gradualist and opportunistic approach, they demanded woman's economic independence, the legalisation of divorce and the expansion of girls' secondary and higher education. Aided by anti-clericalist forces in government they achieved certain successes. In 1879, girls' teacher training colleges were founded; in 1880, women were admitted to lectures at the Sorbonne and a uniform and general system of girls' secondary education established; in 1881, women were allowed to open post office savings accounts in their own names; finally, in 1884 divorce was legalised for the first time since 1816, although it was not until 1938 that married women became independent legal persons. Meanwhile, Josephine Butler, the English moral reformer, had visited Paris in 1874 and aroused some support among Protestants for her international federation against state prostitution. Moral reform was the province of Protestant philanthropists in France and played no immediate part in the rise of radical feminism under Hubertine Auclert. Auclert founded a feminist society, renamed the Women's Suffrage Society in 1883, which aimed to secure for women full equality before the law, equal access to the professions, equal education, equal pay for equal work, divorce and the vote. In her struggles – because of the revolutionary republican French precedents – she employed tactics of demonstration and shadow elections remarkably advanced for the period. Anti-clericalism, however, proved a mixed blessing in this latter part of the struggle as she and her followers encountered determined opposition from Roman Catholic voters. In 1919, however, with Pope Benedict XV's pronouncing in favour of votes for women there was born a Christian feminism. A woman's suffrage bill passed the Chamber of Deputies in 1919 but failed in the Senate in 1922. As late as 1932 extended debates were still taking place on the matter, employing all the old arguments of fifty years before. Only in 1945 did the women of France gain the vote.[22]

In America, the American Revolution did nothing to arrest the decline in female status as the frontier retreated. It was the Second Great Awakening which in particular provided American women with the opportunity to recover lost ground and in its wake came a rapid proliferation of voluntary organisations aimed at moral revival, social reform, education and other general humanitarian objectives. We have already remarked on the connection between feminism and abolitionism. The Grimké sisters, converted from southern Episcopalianism to Quakerism through Presbyterian revivalism shook New England in the 1830's by taking the public platform on the issue of slavery. When, however, the focus of the anti-slavery campaign shifted to congress women, as non-voters,

were deprived of further involvement in the abolitionist cause
and turned their attention elsewhere. Throughout the 1840's they
fought a campaign in New York State for a Married Woman's
Property Bill. It became law in 1848, the year of the Seneca Falls
Convention. A series of conventions followed Seneca Falls, but for
the most part the movement remained unorganised, moderate and
uninterested in the vote. Led by Elizabeth Cady Stanton (of
'Woman's Bible' fame), Susan B. Anthony and including Lucy
Stone and Lucy Mott, they concentrated at first on the economic
subjection of women in civil law. In 1860, a law was passed giving
women in New York the right to collect their own wages, to sue
in court, and to inherit their husband's property. Up until the
Civil War (1861–65) these were the kinds of issues, together with
education, which formed the focal point of the American feminist
movement. During the Civil War these women ceased agitating
and went to the support of the Union in a number of ways. But
in 1866 the Republicans whom they had championed introduced
a Fourteenth Amendment which explicitly denied the vote to
women by insisting that only the freed *male* slaves should be
granted the suffrage. The women were outraged, and from that
time black interests and women's interests diverged. As a result
Stanton founded the National Woman Suffrage Association in
1868. More radical, individualist and anti-clerical in character than
any previous group, it stood for social purity, moral reform and
woman's independence in family life. A statement by Stanton in
1792 justifying the seeking of the franchise sums up well the new
stance:

> The point I wish plainly to bring before you on this occasion
> is the individuality of each human soul; our Protestant idea,
> the right of individual conscience and judgement; our republican
> idea, individual citizenship. In discussing the rights of woman
> we are to consider, first, what belongs to her as an individual,
> in a world of her own, the arbiter of her own destiny, an
> imaginary Robinson Crusoe with her woman Friday on a solitary
> island. Her rights under such circumstances are to use all her
> faculties for her own safety and happiness.

Secondly, if we consider her as a citizen, as a member of a great nation, she must have the same rights as all other members, according to the fundamental principles of our government.

Thirdly, viewed as a woman, an equal factor in civilisation, her rights and duties are still the same: individual happiness and development.

Fourthly, it is only the incidental relations of life, such as mother, wife, sister, daughter, that may involve some special duties and training.[23]

This stance was too radical for some and a breakaway American Woman Suffrage Association was formed in 1868 under the leadership of Lucy Stone. Later they were to unite again in order to propel forward the demand for suffrage.

After the Civil War, a number of women's colleges were opened, so that by 1880 40,000 American women were enrolled in higher education and the best universities such as Harvard and Cornell were admitting women to degrees. In the professions, the pioneering woman physician, Elizabeth Blackwell, founded a hospital in New York in 1857 entirely staffed by women physicians. By 1890 there were no fewer than thirteen medical colleges for women scattered across the States. And even more remarkably, a number of American women entered numerous other professions in the 1870's and 1880's. For instance, by 1880, the United States Supreme Court had admitted a woman to practise at its bar. Likewise, as already mentioned, some denominations were ordaining women to the full ministry of the church. And through a multiplicity of women's organisations, such as university women's associations and professional women's clubs, the influence of feminism began to spread far and wide.

One of the interests taken up by those deprived of the abolitionist platform after the Civil War was the attack on vice, eventually leading to the founding of the American Committee for the Prevention of Legalising Prostitution in 1877. The concern was not new. Since 1834 evangelicals had been deeply involved in the New York Female Moral Reform Society, seeking to convert and change the character of prostitutes. By the 1890's the movement was beginning to achieve many of its objectives. A related concern was that of temperance, leading to the founding of Frances Willard's Women's Christian Temperance Union in 1874. Those involved in the attack on vice or the 'purity campaign' embraced the cause of suffrage in order to further their own ends.

In 1890 the different factions in the feminist movement re-united and began the last stage of the campaign, in the process switching from federal to state tactics. Some encouragement had come with the granting of the vote by the territories of Wyoming and Utah in 1869–70. Eventually, the vote came for all in 1920. But by then America had already gained a worldwide reputation for its feminist vigour.[24]

In Britain, events followed much the same pattern, and British feminism as an organised movement is second only to the American. But the timing in Britain was different, generally speaking, being delayed, although influences such as Mill's *Subjection of Women* were incalculable almost everywhere and Britain's crusade against prostitution under Josephine Butler affected America and France. By the same token, it should not be forgotten that Wesley's revival preceded Finney's and that American revivalism in turn affected Britain in the late nineteenth century.

In the 1850's in Britain, a number of social reforms were made which affected women. In 1852, an Act of Parliament removed a husband's right to enforce cohabitation on his wife. In 1857, a Divorce Act was passed. These, however, were only the beginnings because, until 1891, a husband still had the right to kidnap and imprison his wife, and whereas a man could divorce his wife on grounds of adultery she was obliged to prove him guilty of rape, sodomy or bestiality, or of adultery *in conjunction with* incest, bigamy, cruelty or desertion.

Three main concerns, however, began to dominate as the movement got under way, and as the century progressed these led the movement from a moderate to a more radical position: moral reform, educational opportunity and suffrage.

As early as 1802 William Wilberforce, evangelical anti-slavery campaigner, had founded the Society for the Suppression of Vice to suppress sabbath breaking, blasphemous and lucrative literature, theatres, dancing, fairs, brothels and gaming houses. Considerable effort was expended on protecting the young of both sexes from a knowledge of evil, hence the priority given to censorship. Implicit in the society's aims was belief in male as well as female chastity so that attempts were made to deal with prostitution but without much concern (unlike in New York) for the prostitute as a person. However, Josephine Butler's campaigns after 1869 broke through some of the taboos surrounding the subject. Butler won over the churches and the unions, and finally parliament was persuaded to repeal the Contagious Diseases Act so that in 1883 state regulation of prostitution was suspended and in 1886 abolished altogether. Meanwhile, the Victorian age became increasingly repressive in its attitudes to morality, particularly sexual morality. It resulted in different approaches to reform among liberals and conservatives. The more moderate feminists and the conservatives tended to support repression while the more radical and liberal could not bring themselves to curtail certain individual freedoms. Mill, for example, was for these reasons unable to support sabbatarianism and temperance. The movement for moral reform was on the whole evangelical-inspired and moderately feminist.[25]

On the educational front, the founding of Queen's College for Women (largely inspired by the Christian Socialist, Frederick D. Maurice, only later converted to the woman's cause) in London, in 1848, to be followed in 1849 by Bedford College (under Unitarian auspices and non-denominational in character) gave impetus to a much wider movement for the establishment of an effective secondary education for girls. A Royal Commission Report in 1858 recommended the establishment of a national system of girls' secondary schools to educate middle-class girls for the new, complex and demanding tasks of household management facing the housewife in the expanding society of Victorian England. Unmarried women, incidentally, benefitted as employment opportunities formerly available to marrieds, especially in teaching and medicine, began to close due to an increasing professionalism. Then followed the work of Emily Davies, one of the Langham Place circle, Barbara Leigh Smith and Anne Jemima Clough in the field of higher education: the founding of Girton and Newnham Colleges in Cambridge in the 1870's and the parallel Somerville College and Lady Margaret Hall at Oxford a few years later. First came admission to lectures, then permission to sit examinations without being admitted to degrees and finally degrees, at London in 1880 and followed by the new provincial universities. In the early 1900's Dublin offered degrees to those women who had qualified at Oxford and Cambridge and many women accepted; it was not until 1920 and 1948 respectively that Oxford and Cambridge conferred their degrees on women, many of whom had already won some of their highest honours. Well known for their struggle to obtain nursing and medical qualifications are Florence Nightingale and Elizabeth Garrett Anderson. Women gained the right to register as physicians in 1876 and thereafter nursing and the professions expanded rapidly.[26]

The long hard struggle for the vote began in 1866 with the presentation of a petition in the House of Commons by John Stuart Mill and Henry Fawcett. Following its failure, the National Society for Women's Suffrage was founded in the following year. Its leading figure until 1890 was Lydia Becker, a Manchester liberal, who was followed on her death by the much more radical and militant Millicent Garrett Fawcett. The movement had its ups and downs of dissension and strife, but every year between 1870 and 1878 and from 1884 onwards (with the exception of 1899 and 1901) private members' bills were introduced in parliament. Moderates and radicals, liberals and conservatives aligned themselves differently from time to time according to the party of the government in power and the issues of the day. Conservatives were usually against suffrage on principle and Liberals were very often against it because they feared that women would vote Conservative and also because they had other priorities such as the Irish Question. Yet there was frequently strong parliamentary support and eventually, after the protests of the suffragettes, for which many were sent to prison, and women's part in the war effort, limited suffrage was granted in 1919 and total adult suffrage in 1928.[27] I find it salutary to reflect on what it cost my predecessors to gain what I so easily take for granted.

4. The second wave: equal rights and women's liberation, 1960's–

(i) The onset

When Betty Friedan's *The Feminine Mystique* burst upon the American and British scenes in 1963 it was the occasion rather than the cause of feminism's second wave.[28] It articulated what many individuals and certain groups of women had been feeling for fifteen years and more and gave impetus to a movement. After equal rights before the law had been gained in the 1920's there had followed in Europe and America the Great Depression of the thirties, the World War of the forties and the 'Baby Boom' of the fifties. A few women, especially in the United States, had continued the equal rights struggle to end all discrimination in such areas as marriage, divorce, work, property and jury service.[29] But the campaign for welfare and the fight for access to birth control had gained most women's attention and had, in the case of welfare, for instance, actually militated against women's best interests as a result of protectionism. During the period one important book had appeared, in France: Simone de Beauvoir's classic study of *The Second Sex* appeared in French in 1949 and was translated into English in 1953.

(ii) The issues

Friedan opens her well-argued and persuasively-written analysis of the position of women in Western society with a discussion of the problem 'that has no name'. It is the problem of the middle-class, educated, suburban housewife, caught in the myth of 'the feminine mystique', conditioned by all the consciousness-forming pressures of society to 'desire no greater destiny than to glory in her own femininity'. Not for the truly feminine woman a career, higher education or political rights, not for her the independence and the opportunities which the old-fashioned feminists fought for. To get this message across all the ingenuity of the consumer society was used to portray the enchanting image of the ideal wife and perfect mother.

But somehow the ploy was not working, at least not for the

women. Well-educated, intelligent, accomplished women were like caged birds, living lonely, empty lives in faceless suburbia. They were marrying young and falling apart early.

And so the women's liberation movement was born. Its main aim was to get women back to productive work, which, in the latter part of twentieth-century Western society, meant taking them out of the house. Opposition was swift to come from those who were concerned to keep the traditional or nuclear family intact, with father at work and mother at home, thereby saving the nation from disaster and Western civilisation from collapse! In the process, a new species of woman began to emerge, a kind of androgynous being, neither male nor female but both, and therefore not necessarily intended for relating to the male sex only or to bearing and rearing children. Consequently, not only equal rights before the law but issues like the liberalising of laws relating to homosexuality, contraception and abortion motivated the movement.

In women's liberation the individualist and socialist traditions of feminism had converged, whereas the evangelical had lain dormant. When the voice of evangelicalism was heard it was in the strident tones of 'fundamentalism', speaking out in opposition as the champion of the 'silent majority'. Feminism was beginning to be equated with 'sexual licence' and the 'new morality' whereas fundamentalism increasingly began to look like having a hangover of 'sexual repression' from the Victorian era.[30]

(iii) The achievements

The solid achievements, after twenty years of hard labour, have been, in my opinion, minimal. Laws relating to marriage, divorce, homosexuality, abortion and birth control have been liberalised in a number of countries. And in Britain, the Sex Discrimination Act was passed in 1975. But equality before the law is not enough, as past experience has only too clearly shown. Some form of 'positive discrimination' appears to be called for. In America, the National Organisation for Women (NOW) fought a long and hard campaign under its blunt and tenacious president, Eleanor Smeal, to have the Equal Rights Amendment to the Constitution (ERA) ratified.

Ten years earlier in 1972 ERA had been passed by congress, but in the America of 1982 it failed by a margin of three to be ratified by the states. A combination of the 'feminine', adroit, campaigning Phyllis Schlafly and groups such as the Eagle Forum, the John Birch Society, Fundamentalist Christian churches, the Moral Majority and the Mormon Church had succeeded in playing to people's worst fears, by miring down the fight in 'dire warnings of homosexual marriages and unisex toilets'.[31] The 'silent majority' had already been conditioned by the feminine mystique created by popular books and lecture courses like Marabel Morgan's on the 'Total Woman'. Even Betty Friedan, in her most recent book, *The Second Stage*, admits that the feminist movement ignored 'women's deep-rooted feelings about marriage and the family'. In seeking to begin to redress the balance she calls for less narcissism in the next stage of the movement and a commitment to make 'the family the new feminist frontier'.[32]

At first, some gains were achieved in the areas of equal pay and equal opportunities, but recent statistics show a distinct decline in woman's position: there is a down-turn in the graph. Moreover, as the recession of the eighties deepens and the unemployment figures soar, already voices may be heard demanding that women go back home in order to make way for the men at work.

Conclusions

The origins of feminism may be identified in three traditions which arose during the eighteenth and nineteenth centuries: egalitarianism, evangelicalism and socialism. Its aims may be stated as concern for equal rights before the law necessitating major social and moral reform or, in the case of the socialists, revolution. Of the three countries briefly considered only France did not have a well-organised feminist movement and only France did not experience a major evangelical revival; what organisation there was, however, owed a great deal to a few Protestant activists and philanthropists.

I wish to suggest that the evangelical tradition contributed in a major way to the early development of feminism. But I also wish to argue that the tendency to sexual repression in the Victorian era and the threat which radical feminism of a socialist kind posed to the nuclear family and traditional values, together with an increasingly fundamentalistic, literalist interpretation of the Scriptural injunction that a wife should obey her husband contributed to evangelicals and feminists parting company. More recently, in feminism's second wave, a few evangelicals are beginning to rediscover their own feminist heritage; most, however, are still confused, because of the inferred threat to the family and challenge to biblical authority posed by feminism.

Part Three:

LOOKING TO THE FUTURE

6: **The image restored**
Woman and personhood

For years I had followed a daily Bible-reading plan and while at college I had studied many books of the Bible both academically and devotionally. In addition I had often turned to the Psalms and the Epistles for extra spiritual sustenance. But I can truthfully say that no reading of the Scriptures made as great an impression on my life and consciousness as that which began with the daily teaching of the Gospels for seven years in a Third World country. Perhaps the setting of Kenya then was closer to the Palestine of Jesus' day than my own industrialised, depersonalised, Western culture. Or perhaps the issues with which Jesus dealt appeared more directly relevant to Kenyans' needs. I don't know. But I do know that the life and ministry of Jesus became alive and significant for me in a new way. I began to appreciate for the first time the meaning of the incarnation as well as the atonement, of Jesus' life as much as his death, God coming into the world and identifying with needy humankind.

I marvelled how Jesus was able to communicate with all kinds and conditions in his encounters with people and more particularly how he always respected the integrity and dignity of the person, the inherent value and rights of the individual made in God's image. But you may well ask what I mean by the word 'person' and the concept of 'personhood' in such a context. And I must reply – as a look at any dictionary will readily confirm – that the task of definition is not an easy one. From ancient times, a person has been defined as 'an individual substance of a rational nature', and Man has been distinguished from the rest of the animals on that account. The Hebrews may be said to have developed and modified the idea while conceiving Man to be made in the image and likeness of God. In our earlier discussion we said that the

godlikeness of Man may be identified in the beauty and perfection
of his physical form and in his spiritual powers of thought, communication and self-transcendence. By virtue of this correspondence,
Man differs from the animals and is destined for a personal
relationship with his Maker and for an intermediary role in creation.[1] And it is this capacity for personal relationship which is
characteristic of human nature – it is what makes us human. It is
perhaps worth noting in passing that the generic term 'Man'
includes the male and the female, as does the word 'person'. With
regard to what it means to be a person, Paul Tournier, Swiss
Christian psychologist and physician, expresses it well and
succinctly when he writes: 'Being a person means assuming
responsibility for oneself, responding to one's inner vocation, freely
choosing one's goals in life, and the routes one wishes to take to
achieve them.'[2] Jesus encountered many people who, in his society,
were regarded as non-persons, as having few if any human rights,
and gave them back their freedom and self-respect: tax-collectors,
prostitutes, freedom-fighters, foreigners, women, the sick and the
possessed. He had come, he said, not to call the righteous but
sinners to repentance.

1. Jesus and the personhood of woman

Further explorations still into the Gospels, led me, as already
intimated, to discover how totally unconventional Jesus was in his
attitude to women. And even more recently I have been impressed
by the women's response to Jesus. It would appear that his treating
of them as persons in their own right elicited from them a profound
personal response. The story of how he was anointed by women
on two occasions and the way the accounts of the incidents have
been misinterpreted and misconstrued from early times provides
a fascinating example.

All four Evangelists tell the story of a woman who anoints Jesus
with ointment. The setting and some of the details, however,
vary from one account to another, causing not a little scholarly
confusion. The most satisfactory resolution of the problem is to

recognise that Mark and Luke recount two basically separate incidents and that Matthew and John play variations on their themes.

According to Mark, the passion is approaching and Jesus is at table in the house of Simon the leper at Bethany. A woman with an alabaster flask of very expensive ointment comes up to Jesus, breaks the flask and pours the ointment over his head. Immediately, some of those present indignantly ask why expensive ointment – which might have been sold for the equivalent of a labourer's yearly earnings and the proceeds given to the poor – should be thus wasted. At the same time they reproach the woman. But Jesus tells them to leave her alone because she has done something beautiful for him. They will always have the poor with them; they will not always have him. This woman has done what she could; she anointed his body beforehand for burying and her deed will be recalled in her memory wherever the gospel is preached in the world (Mark 14.3–9).

According to Luke, Jesus is still in Galilee, during the early period of his ministry, at table in the house of Simon the Pharisee. A woman of the city, a sinner (probably a prostitute), hearing where he is, comes into the house, bringing an alabaster flask of ointment. She stands behind the reclining Jesus, 'at his feet', weeping. Her tears soon begin to wet his feet, so she wipes them dry with her hair, kisses them and anoints them with the ointment. Whereupon, Simon the Pharisee, the host, protests: if Jesus 'were a prophet, he would have known who and what sort of woman this is who is touching him, for she is a sinner'. Jesus' reply is to tell the parable of the two debtors and compel Simon to admit that the one who has been forgiven most will love the more. He then turns and contrasts Simon's actions with the woman's: 'I entered your house, you gave me no water for my feet, but she has wet my feet with her tears and wiped them with her hair. You gave me no kiss, but from the time I came in she has not ceased to kiss my feet. You did not anoint my head with oil, but she has anointed my feet with ointment' (Luke 7.36–50).

According to John, it is Mary of Bethany who, six days before his passion, anoints Jesus' feet with expensive ointment and it is

Judas Iscariot, the traitorous disciple – 'a thief' – who protests that the proceeds should have been given to the poor (John 12.1–8).

Matthew's account follows Mark's to all intents and purposes (Matt. 26.6–13).

But, we may ask, what light do these incidents throw on the subject of a woman's personhood?

Firstly, it is fascinating to explore how Christian history, liturgy and art have interpreted them. Already in John, the hitherto 'unnamed woman' is named as Mary of Bethany. Then, in the fourth century, a Syrian church Father called Ephraem identifies this Mary with Mary of Magdala – the Magdalene, out of whom Jesus had cast seven demons and who was the first to witness the risen Christ (Mark 16.9–11; John 20.14–18) – who is in turn believed to be the same person as the sinful woman or prostitute of Luke's story (Luke 7.37). And from the time of Pope Gregory the Great, the liturgy of the Roman Catholic Church, similarly 'rolling all three into one', honours them in a single feast.[3] The confusion is compounded and continued in Christian art. Usually, a woman, obviously a repentant sinner, is portrayed weeping at the Lord's feet, drying them with her falling tresses and anointing them with oil. She is Mary Magdalene, symbol of fallen and rescued womanhood. Only rarely, as in the case of a thirteenth-century illustration for a Psalter in a Cistercian Convent in Basel, is the woman depicted as anointing Jesus' head. There, at the Last Supper, dressed in nun's garb, she is seen standing behind Jesus, pouring oil on his head; yet at the same time another woman, obviously a sinner, is under the table wiping his feet with the undone locks of her hair. Elisabeth Moltmann-Wendel suggests that 'the humble, servile attitude of anointing the feet had suppressed an ancient, early Christian recollection.'[4] Perhaps the nuns, who may have either commissioned or even executed the painting themselves, were arriving at a sense of independence and self-awareness.

Secondly, the meaning and significance of the incidents have been much debated by commentators. Suffice it to make a few simple suggestions here. The 'unnamed prostitute' was expressing to Jesus heartfelt gratitude for his acceptance of her as a person.

Such were the depths of her feelings that she was willing to burst in upon an all-male gathering in the house of a Pharisee with her offering of love. Perhaps she approached Jesus from behind in order to anoint his head, but was so overcome by emotion that she wept for her sins on his feet, undid her tresses to wipe them and before she knew what she was doing she had broken the flask and poured out the ointment – for there is no precedent for anointing a person's feet. It is also possible that the second 'unnamed woman' understood – better than the unbelieving disciples, who were still expecting Jesus to establish an earthly kingdom and two of whom had just requested positions of power – that Jesus' mission was to suffer and to die. As Samuel the prophet had been entrusted by God with the anointing of Saul (and later, David) as king so, too, this unknown woman, anticipating Jesus' death, anoints the Messiah, consecrates him and equips him for his task. As Moltmann-Wendel says: 'This is a twofold break with the patriarchal tradition: the king is a candidate for death and Israel is under foreign rule, and an anonymous woman takes on the role of the "men of Judah" (II Sam. 2.4). Here is the proclamation of a new age in which old values will be turned upside down.'[5] Perhaps, too, there is even an anticipation of resurrection.

Thus it is that women, treated by Jesus as persons, respond with the understanding and faith which arise out of the depths of real personal encounter. And so it is that they, rather than the twelve disciples, show an extraordinary and extravagant appreciation of his person, foresee his death and first witness his resurrection.

2. Restoring the image

Paul Tournier tells of a woman journalist, Michèle Perrein, whose account of an important vice trial was turned down. 'I had done something one must not do,' she says, 'I had written it as a woman. Not the sort of woman's article that newspaper editors expect – full of trivialities – but a real woman's article, because I was judging as a woman, in the same way as editors do when they judge as men.' She adds, 'Had I been a man, no doubt my article would have been accepted.' One of the many experiments carried out on such attitudes confirms her judgment: 'Two hundred female students were invited to judge a philosophical essay. The first hundred were given an essay signed "John MacKay"; the remaining hundred were given the same essay, but signed "Joan MacKay". John's work, in the vast majority of cases, was found to be original, profound, and imaginative. That of Joan was considered to be superficial, commonplace, and uninteresting.'[6] I am reminded of the many committees on which I have served, the suggestions made which at the time, I felt, were not taken seriously, only to re-appear in a male guise and be implemented.

But when I encounter Jesus I always feel that he takes me and other women seriously: I am affirmed as a person and as a woman.

What Jesus does, it seems to me, is to act as if the image of God in Man can be restored, indeed has been in certain circumstances. Remember how, when the Pharisees approached him to ask whether or not it was unlawful for a man to divorce his wife, Jesus appealed to God's intention from the beginning of creation? Referring to a time before the fall he says: 'From the beginning of creation, "God made them male and female. For this reason a man shall leave his father and mother and be joined to his wife, and the two shall become one." So they are no longer two but one' (Mark 10.6–8). Similarly, Paul can affirm that in Christ Jesus – in the new creation – there is no male and female; all are one (Gal. 3.28). All the barriers created by society in order to discriminate between men and women have been broken down in the new creation, initiated in and through Jesus Christ.

An even more sobering thought (in one sense; exhilarating in another) is that Christ is the firstborn of all creation, 'the image of the unseen God' (Col. 1.15–20). Therefore, by his incarnation in Jesus, the Second Adam, he is demonstrating how God relates to women. God takes me seriously as a person; and my Christian calling, like any man's, is 'to be conformed to the image of his Son' (Rom. 8.29).

3. Persons and things

Whereas Elisabeth Elliot's *Let Me Be a Woman* makes me laugh
one minute, cry the next, with incredulity coupled with indigna-
tion, and at the end shrug my shoulders while agreeing with a
reviewer who remarked, 'Methinks the woman doth protest too
much!' not so Marabel Morgan's bestseller, *The Total Woman*.[7]
Despite all I had been led to expect I was unprepared for my
reaction: I was in turn shocked, impressed and, at the end, deeply
disturbed, especially when I reflected on the enormous influence
of her courses in the subject. At first I was not quite sure why. I
had a hunch, a gut-reaction, which I could not easily articulate.
But upon further reflection, aided by some reading, I began to
understand why I was worried and attempted to assess the implications of what I had discerned.

A synopsis of Morgan's book would read something like this.
After several years of marriage to Charlie, Marabel was coming to
the conclusion that their marriage was much less than the superla-
tive experience she had hoped for and began to search for an
answer to the problem. With humour and candour she recalls the
carefree days of courtship when Charlie was 'a voracious talker'
and she was mesmerised by the 'marvellous communication'
between them. Very soon, however, Charlie stopped talking and
as the years wore on things got worse. Each evening, when Charlie
walked in the front door after work, a cloud of gloom and tension
flowed in with him. And although Marabel had waited all day 'to
love and care for him' they were soon 'at each other' for no known
reason. Their evenings usually ended up with Charlie 'sprawled'
before the television set and Marabel hating every moment of their
existence. Eventually, one evening, it all came to a head. Charlie
arrived home from work, to reveal his plans for the following
evening. But Marabel already had hers; she protested and he
exploded. Marabel, he said, always challenged him on every decision which he made. And while she vehemently denied all allega-
tions, he proceeded to lay down the law: 'From now on when I
plan for us to go somewhere, I will tell you twenty minutes ahead

of time. You'll have time to get ready, and we'll do without all the crying!'[8]

Thus began Marabel's search for advice on how to go about repairing her marriage and her consequent discovery of the 'Total Woman' concept. Quite simply, she came to the conclusion that she was not accepting her husband as he was. This is how she expresses it: 'Your man needs to feel important, loved and accepted. If you won't accept his idiosyncrasies, who will? A Total Woman caters to her man's special quirks, whether it be in salads, sex, or sports. She makes his home his haven, a place to which he can run. She allows him that priceless luxury of unqualified acceptance.' This means responding to his every exciting idea with a, 'Yes, let's!' because, 'It is only when a woman surrenders her life to her husband, reveres and worships him and is willing to serve him, that she becomes really beautiful to him. She becomes a priceless jewel, the glory of femininity, his queen!'[9]

But even such capitulation and a new method of organising her time and managing the household were not enough. She had to compete with the 'girls in the office' for her husband's attentions and affections. So she describes how she soaked her body in a warm sweet-smelling bubble bath, donned pink baby-doll pyjamas and white boots, and waltzed to the door to greet her husband 'in a cloud of powder and cologne', cooing softly, 'I crave your body'. For man's most basic needs are warm sexual love, approval and admiration.[10] A woman must (she had decided): *accept* her husband just as he is; *admire* her husband every day; *adapt* to his way of life, accepting his friends, his food and his life-style; and *appreciate* all he does for her.

The concept was a roaring success. Not only did Marabel's and Charlie's marriage become blissfully happy, but all the married couples in Charlie's football club joined one of her first classes in Miami, adopted what had by now developed into a system and the very next season won all their matches and became world champions.[11]

So why am I worried, if the 'Total Woman' concept spells such marital success and the book contains much sound and wise advice on husband-wife relations, sexual fulfilment and bringing up children? I have two basic concerns. The first is that the attitude of submissiveness adopted by Marabel to her husband, Charlie, is one enjoined on each Christian in relation to another. So where does that leave Charlie? The second and perhaps more serious reservation is that Marabel reduces herself to a mere 'sex-object' by denying her own value as a person, with a will of her own. As I hope to show later, both concerns involve the personhood of the man as well as the woman: Charlie's personhood is as much at risk as Marabel's. But before I draw my own conclusions I wish to share the comments and observations of two other writers.

Writing as a feminist, Betty Friedan observes in *The Second Stage*:

> So Phyllis Schlafly and Marabel Morgan make a lot of money pursuing their own careers, going around the country lecturing to women that they don't need equal rights, just husbands to support them (which they'll allegedly stop doing when the Equal Rights Amendment is passed).[12] But Phyllis Schlafly is herself taking advantage of the equal opportunity she says other women don't need, getting her law degree at a prestigious university which never would have admitted a middle-aged woman like herself before the women's movement. And Marabel Morgan admits to *Time* magazine that she herself no longer has time to deck her naked body in Saran Wrap, ostrich feathers, black-lace garter belt and baby-white boots, in the manner she prescribes to all those insecure women who pay her for lessons on how to meet their tired husbands at the door, cooing, 'I crave your body,' to keep them from straying and to keep themselves supported in the style they'd like to stay accustomed to. Marabel Morgan's ability now to contribute her own money to that support may be assumed to be as enticing to her own husband as the Saran Wrap, which in real life does not seem to keep those husbands from straying. Lecturing in Texas recently, several months after Marabel Morgan ran one of her 'Total Woman' courses, I heard from some psychologists of the devastation to women, who had flogged themselves on to new depths of self-degradation and denial with those ostrich

feathers and Saran Wrap maneuvers, when their husbands, in fact, did run off (maybe faster?) with the younger 'chicks' from the office.[13]

Writing as a psychologist and general medical practitioner who believes that women have a mission in the world related to their greater 'sense of the person' and 'gift of feeling' and commenting on the Total Woman's 'Yes, let's!' principle Paul Tournier observes:

If I understand properly, that means complete capitulation, the very opposite of the claims of the feminists, and in a categorical form which I do not remember having met elsewhere. She repeats several times: 'It pays.' And she shows that it works: not only did their conjugal bliss become cloudless, but their happiness was contagious. . . . Jolly good for them, but for my part I should not have wanted to marry a woman who was so little of a person on her own account.

Yes, my wife accepted me, and I felt it. But when she did not agree with me she told me so clearly and sometimes explosively. This led us to take a different road to happiness, that of dialogue. The sky is not cloudless along that road, but it is a factor of growth for each of the partners. Was it not dialogue that was missing when Marabel Morgan was tense, irritated, and silent? Nevertheless, in justice it must be said that her book abounds in observations and advice full of wisdom.

It was not her husband who exacted that sort of submission from Marabel Morgan. She adopted it freely herself, as a person. There is a certain paradox here: of her own accord she chose once and for all to stifle her personal reactions. [I am not so sure that Tournier is altogether correct here.]

It also has a certain grandeur. But is she accomplishing her mission, in the sense in which I use the word in this book? She lets her husband decide everything, do anything he likes. Is not this willing submission precisely the course adopted by women in past centuries? We are seeing now the result of that

– a masculine world that functions like a piece of machinery, with no regard paid to emotional reactions.

Our grandmothers did not imagine it possible to adopt any other attitude, since there was no other model to follow. Whereas Marabel Morgan knows that she could act differently, and she would certainly have the courage to do so. She herself says, 'I am by nature rather dictatorial.' That is perhaps the key to the book: it is those who are naturally dictatorial who have most to gain from the experience of abdication. However that may be, my reaction to this book was to reflect that I should have been rather humiliated if my wife had adopted such a tactic, and if she alone had deserved the credit for our mutual understanding. On reflection, I am prouder than Mr Morgan.[14]

My perception that Marabel Morgan had reduced herself to a mere 'sex-object' led me to look once again at Martin Buber's concept of the 'I – Thou' (or 'I – You') and 'I – It' relationships.[15] In a nutshell, Buber claims that people enter into two kinds of relationships, the 'I – You' relationship of personal reciprocity or the 'I – It' relationship of objective or scientific analysis. We may enter into the 'I – You' relationship with nature (for example, either with a tree, as poets have been wont to do, or as did St Francis of Assisi, with 'brother sun'), with other persons and above all and most perfectly and unconditionally with God, the absolute You. In the 'I – You' relationship personhood is maximised by reciprocity or mutuality. In the 'I – It' relationship personhood is diminished by objectivity. Thus, in paradoxical fashion, Charlie helps to diminish his own personhood by relating to his wife as a 'sex-object' – a means to an end rather than an end in herself – while Marabel maximises hers by relating to her husband as a person. She, too, however, could be in danger of using her husband as a means of achieving marital bliss rather than seeking to relate to him as a person. A relationship cannot be truly personal until it becomes a mutual, reciprocal partnership between two equal persons. This is what is meant by equality in marriage and equality between the sexes. Differences and distinctions are not precluded. Moroever, God is never an 'It', he is eternally and always 'You' – subject and object, but never a thing. And if men and women are to mirror God they must relate to each other as persons and never as things, never as means towards an end, be the end ever so noble. Thus the personhood of woman precludes her being treated as any man's property.

4. Thinking and feeling

It is quite common to equate cool rational thought, clear-headed logic, with maleness or the masculine principle and warm emotional feelings, fuzzy-headed intuition, with femaleness or the feminine principle. And because Western society has been dominated by reason since the Renaissance it is possible to classify it as a society devoted to masculine roles and values, which must therefore despise and reject women. Paul Tournier holds that the solution to the demise of Western civilisation consequently lies with enabling woman, somehow, to return to the world of affairs where she can contribute to healing the malaise through her special 'gift of feeling'. Significantly, Tournier the physician is able to make his appeal only because he accepts the findings of one school of psychology and follows the wisdom of a particular current of philosophical thought. He affirms the psychologist, C. G. Jung's, universal archetypes of the *animus* and *anima* (respectively the contrasexual components in men and women) and follows the Chinese principle of the *Yin* and the *Yang* (the complementary and harmonising tendencies of the positive and negative, active and passive, masculine and feminine in men and women). Similarly, Elisabeth Elliot is able to identify for her nephew 'the mark of a man' because she believes that 'biologically' and 'mysteriously' man is different from woman. She writes to Pete:

> Last week I thought of you again, at a student convention where I was speaking . . . . I realized how badly things have gotten twisted in the past decade or so, when – apropos of my thesis that there *is* a difference between men and women, that they're not interchangeable – I called for a show of hands of the men who would like to be asked for a date. I was quite unprepared

for the response. Hundreds of hands went up. I should have asked then to see the hands of those who would *not* want to be asked (I wonder if there would have been any), but I was too startled and confused. When I suggested that we post a sign-up sheet at the back of the auditorium, the clapping, cheering, and shrieking (loudest, I suppose, from the single women) was tumultuous. Everybody but me was amused. Children of their time, so accustomed to hearing about *equality* and *rights* and *personhood*, they no longer know what the difference *is* between the sexes. They even wonder whether it is legitimate to notice any difference or whether it might not be better to pretend there is none.

Well, Pete, there is one. . . .
The biological difference is – so far, at least – an undeniable datum. There is a certain 'unbudgeableness' about simple facts. They won't go away. But science is working hard to change all that. God helps us if it succeeds! . . .

There *is* a difference besides the biological one. . . .

'You mean all those tired old stereotypes: Men are supposed to do this; women are supposed to do that? Nothing but conditioning! . . .'

No, Pete. I'm not talking about biology or stereotypes or social ideologies. I'm talking about what sexuality (masculinity and femininity) *means*. Ever stop to wonder if the physiology means anything? . . .

There is a mystery. It's this mystery that I wanted to write about for you. You are a man, Pete, and I know it when I see you. I thank God for your manliness.

And she continues to define manliness, over against femininity, as taking the initiative rather than making a response and as exercising authority rather than submitting in obedience. Man's gifts are initiative and leadership ability, woman's roles are responsiveness and subordination.[16]

But how can they be sure – sages, philosophers, popularising theologians and psychologists, even Freud with his theory that female sexuality is determined by penis-envy in the young girl –

either of the diagnosis or the cure? Well, they cannot. Modern
research is beginning to demonstrate not only wide divergences of
opinion among the different schools of psychology but also the
incomplete state of present scientific knowledge. The three main
points at issue and of relevance and interest have already been
brought into focus by our quotations: (i) the various theories as to
how men develop into men and women develop into women; (ii)
the ways by which men do or do not differ from women and
vice versa; (iii) and the nature, function and interchangeability of
masculine and feminine roles in society.[17]

First, how do men develop into men and women into women?
Radical feminists have always maintained that social conditioning
(or the environment) alone is responsible for determining what
we have come to perceive as characteristically male and female
behaviour. At the other extreme anti-feminists and biological deter-
minists maintain that biology – that is, physiological and hormonal
differences alone – determines the obvious differences between the
sexes. Modern research points us in the direction of a both/and
rather than an either/or solution: both nature and nurture are to
be taken into account together with the effects of interaction
between the two. Moreover, exciting insights are being gained
from current research on the importance of a child's self-percep-
tion, its personal classification of his or her own sexual identity.

Second, to what extent, if any, do the sexes differ? Apart from
the biological differences, such as male strength, life expectancy,
the reproductive organs and the procreative functions, there are
few which can be absolutely and uniformly identified. There is
some well-established evidence to show that women have the slight
edge over men in verbal ability and that boys excel in visual and
spatial tasks and at a later age in mathematical skills. But the
difference is not constant and there are some indications that
environmental as well as hereditary factors, nurture as well as
nature, play a part in the process of development.

Third, can we identify distinctive and definitive masculine and
feminine roles, describe their function and declare them fixed,
or could it be possible that such roles are interchangeable? The
stereotypes are well-known: women are more patient, more

emotional, more intuitive, more dependent; and they are often illogical, curious, vain or flippant. Men are assertive, creative, ambitious, more independent; and possibly more intelligent, or, certainly more rational and logical. And, quite naturally, their different characteristics suit them for their divergent roles. Listen to a verse from 'A Hymn to Him' in *My Fair Lady*, the musical version of Shaw's *Pygmalion*:

> Women are irrational, that's all there is to that!
> Their heads are full of cotton, hay and rags!
> They're nothing but exasperating, irritating, vacillating,
>   calculating, agitating, maddening and infuriating hags!
> Why can't a woman be more like a man?
> Men are so honest, so thoroughly square;
> Eternally noble, historically fair;
> Who, when you win, will always give your back a pat!
> Why can't a woman be like that?[18]

Recent research has analysed in great detail how a culture's role expectations affect the individual. For instance, when a man is compelled to act in an 'unmanly' way and a woman in a manner which is considered 'unfeminine' how do they react to the pressures? To date, the findings indicate that obviously individuals cope in different ways: some adjust, others rebel, some are not aware that there is any pressure and others become over-sensitive. So the research continues.

What then may we conclude about sex and gender differences? Hereditary and environmental factors both play a part in determining differences, but as to the final nature of role distinctions we must keep an open mind, because of the, as yet, less than fully-understood effects of role-stereotyping. Meanwhile, the most recent and comprehensive research tends to confirm neither prejudice nor rigid stereotyping, but to point in the direction of a common humanity, bisexual in nature yet in many respects still a mystery defying explanation.

Conclusions

And so to make some concluding remarks about woman and personhood.

First, I believe that neither a culturally-conditioned theology nor the findings of modern psychology can be validly used to make extravagant claims either by feminists or their opponents. What little we do know for certain on the subject indicates the need for caution and a more open-ended approach, while at the same time pointing in certain directions.

Second, I believe that Jesus, both by his flouting of social conventions and his breaking of religious taboos, tegether with his explicit teaching on the matter (thereby denying rigid role-stereotyping and certain rabbinic interpretations of the Old Testament Scriptures), reclaimed for woman her nature and dignity as a person, created equally with man in the image and likeness of God.

Third, and very significantly, I believe that a person is Man in his totality and unity as body, mind and spirit, and in his bisexuality as male and female or man and woman together. True personhood is therefore realised in the complementarity of man and woman and in their relationship with nature, their fellows and God. God meant it to be like that, says Jesus, from the beginning from the moment God willed the creation of humankind.[19]

7: Heirs to Martha
Women in the home

'Jesus came to Bethany. . . . There they made him a supper;
Martha served.'

(John 12.2)

'Martha said to Jesus, 'Yes, Lord; I believe that you are the Christ, the
Son of God, he who is coming into the world.'

(John 11.27)

Mary and Martha have always fascinated me. You may recall how
I was driven to examine the biblical text and its context in order
to satisfy my curiosity as to why Jesus seemed to commend Mary's
behaviour while rebuking Martha for hers. I was not happy with
the traditional tendency to exalt Mary as the type of the contemplative Christian and Martha as her active counterpart. How exhilarating then to discover through Elisabeth Moltmann-Wendel's *The
Women around Jesus* that the church has preserved two distinct
traditions about Martha.[1] The first features Martha the home-
maker, the busy housewife who 'serves', a type of the active Christian who is full of good works. The second exalts Martha the
Christian leader, the strong active woman, full of faith and wisdom
as well as good works. Both traditions reflect in some measure the
image portrayed by Luke and John (Luke 10.38–42; John 11.1–44,
12.1–8), where the temperaments and characteristics of the two
sisters of Bethany are compared and contrasted in remarkably
similar fashion. And one commentator hints at tradition's pictures
of Martha when he comments: 'John conveys a wonderfully lifelike
portrait of a faithful but rather managing woman.'[2]

1. Martha the housewife and Martha the woman

There are no hymns about Martha. 'Because she went into the
kitchen to prepare a meal for Jesus, her guest,' says Moltmann-
Wendel, 'she has been relegated to cooking and housekeeping.'[3]
For this reason, too, she becomes the patron saint of housewives
and cooks, and is given a saint's day (29 July) as such. Similarly,
she provides a suitable image for 'active women' like social workers
and deaconesses. And even nowadays one finds Martha organisations devoted to domestics in manses and guest-houses and Martha
movements dedicated to opposing the emancipation of women.
Moreover, since the time of the Reformers, numerous Bible
commentators use the active Martha as a warning to those who
would seek to be made righteous by their good works: it is quite
wrong that Martha should seek to do something for Jesus because
salvation is a free gift of God made available by grace through
faith (Eph. 2.8–10). And it is the homely, practical Martha who
is most often portrayed in Christian art. She is the patron saint of
those who nurse the sick because she is practical and caring. In
these roles she is depicted as a housekeeper with a key-ring and
as a cook in a great Dutch Renaissance kitchen and, in a little
half-ruined Martha church above Lugano, she is portrayed as a
nurse dressed in white, dedicating a group of lay brothers to the
care of those suffering from the plague.

This is the Martha who serves, who pours out her 'self' in the
service of others. In the eyes of many she is quintessential woman.

But there is another Martha, the Martha who is modelled after
the woman who goes out to meet Jesus in order to make a request
concerning her brother, Lazarus. 'If you had been here,' she says
to Jesus, 'my brother would not have died. And even now I know
that whatever you ask from God, God will give you.' This elicits
from Jesus the response, 'Your brother will rise again.' But Martha
replies, 'I know that he will rise again in the resurrection at the
last day.' And, perhaps to encourage a personal engagement, Jesus
makes one of his great 'I am' pronouncements, followed by a
question, 'I am the resurrection and the life; he who believes in
me, though he die, yet shall he live, and whoever lives and believes

n me shall never die. Do you believe this?' 'Yes, Lord;' confesses
Martha, 'I believe that you are the Christ, the Son of God, he who
s coming into the world' (John 11.21–7). This 'other' Martha is
he one who, like Peter, confesses who Jesus is: the 'Christ', the
Son of God' and the 'coming one' – three christological titles.

This 'other' Martha is preserved by tradition as a mature
woman, full of Christian faith, strong, competent and organising
– an apostle of the early church. With her sister Mary and her
brother Lazarus she is believed to have been expelled from
Palestine and set adrift on a raft. Arriving in France, all three
became missionaries. And it is in the south of France that the
legend and cult of Martha, the faithful and strong Christian leader,
emerges amidst the women's movements of the high middle ages
and among the Dominicans whose founder, Domenicus, always
worked with women, seeking to win them away from 'heretical'
circles. In the Christian art of the fourteenth and fifteenth centuries, Martha appears as the spiritual and competent one, often in
contrast to her sister who is by now Mary Magdalene: Martha
becomes the 'great mother' as over against Mary who is the 'great
sinner'. And in Fra Angelico, the Dominican painters' 'Geth-
semane', in the monastery of San Marco in Florence, Martha
watches with Jesus, praying with uplifted hands and casting questioning glances at her sister, while Mary reads a book with head
bowed and the three disciples, Peter, James and John, sleep
soundly.[4] Similarly, in another painting, Fra Angelico represents
Martha as the only woman alongside St Veronica, beneath the
cross.[5]

Another medieval image of Martha depicts her defeating the
dragon, not violently with a sword, like St George, but in the form
of a mature woman, nun or elegant young society lady binding
him with a cross or fettering him with her girdle. The dragon is
the symbol of evil par excellence. All the biblical beasts which
symbolise evil, says Moltmann-Wendel, are united in the dragon:
the serpent, the apocalyptic dragon, the beast from the abyss.
Moreover, as the dragon is frequently shown to have a woman's
face, it is highly significant that Martha, the mature Christian
woman, faithful and courageous, should herself achieve victory

over the dragon. It is as if the woman, confronted with her like, conquers that which is feared by women. Again, to quote: 'The evaluation of women in negative terms, in terms of chaos, is abolished. Patriarchal mythology ends in a biblical, Christian figure.'[6] And it is significant that the theme of Martha and the dragon reached its high point in the feminist culture of the Renaissance. Thereafter, it gave way to the patriarchal St George figure, key symbol of the *militia Christi*.

For present purposes, the divergent traditions about Martha aptly and succinctly sum up the dilemma of Christian woman today. Is woman's primary, proper, womanly and feminine calling one of service to humankind as a good wife and mother and only secondarily, if at all, one of fulfilling her potential as a person whom God may use as he sees fit? Or, to put the question in another way, perhaps more starkly, am I as a single woman, pursuing a career, missing out on what is best and are my married friends who have chosen not to have children pursuing an abnormal course? What is woman's true vocation? I happen to believe (and have already laid the foundations of my argument in earlier chapters of this book) that although these kinds of questions may be posed they are misplaced. In the future we shall resolve the dilemma.

2. The family past and present

A popular topic of conversation nowadays is the family. And the vagaries of women seem to constitute the gravest of threats to its existence and well-being. Christian and non-Christian alike express concern about the breakdown of the family unit and the consequent demise of family life. Yet I believe that so much of the sentiment underlying such freely expressed opinions is based on misinformation and incorrect assumptions that it can fairly be said to be nonsensical. But, you may well ask, in what respect? And I shall reply with the simple observation that both historically and culturally the concept 'family' has meant different things to different peoples for a variety of reasons. Even in my own limited

experience I have encountered diverse kinds of marriage and *No!*
several forms of family life.

The family is society's basic unit or key institution. Every record
of early man reveals evidence of family life. It functions as a
socially approved sex relationship, characterised by various rights
and obligations. By way of comprehensive definition it may be
said to consist of one or more women living with one or more
men and their children. The major kinds of marriage relationship
observed, in order of their comparative incidence, are as follows:
monogamy (one man and one woman), polygyny (one man with
two or more wives), polyandry (one woman with two or more
husbands) and group marriage. Common residence and economic
co-operation are usually associated with the family and frequently
a family's reproductive functions are secondary to its wider economic and social functions.

The family unit may take numerous and varied forms in order
to function socially and economically as well as reproductively.
Mention of the most important will serve to give us some idea of
the complexity of the issue. The *nuclear* family comprises a married
couple with their children. The *composite* family is made up of at
least two related nuclear families in one household; but may consist
of several individual families, such as a man and his sons' families,
or a man with several wives, living in one household. The *conjugal*
family (sometimes called the small family or the biological family)
is a nucleus of spouses surrounded by a fringe of relatives; it is the
husband-wife-children relationship which is functionally primary,
while the other individuals remain subordinate. The *extended*
family consists of a series of close relatives along either the male
or female line but rarely both; for example, either a woman and
her husband with their children, some of whom are married daughters with husbands or a man and his wife with their children, some
of whom are married sons with wives. The *consanguineal* family is
an extended family where the husband-wife-children relationship
is functionally subordinate to the father-son or mother-daughter
relationship.[7] And so we might go on. Enough has been said,
however, to indicate that when we complain about the breakdown
of family life in the West today we do not differentiate precisely

enough between the different kinds of marriage possible and the forms taken by family life as a result. What we usually mean is that we regret and deplore the replacing of life-long monogamy by what may be termed either serial monogamy or successive polygamy and the resulting breakup of the nuclear family unit comprising 'Mum, Dad and the kids'. Moreover, Christians make a further assumption still by equating what Edward Shorter calls the 'modern' family (monogamous and nuclear) with the biblical and therefore the Christian. Many of the Old Testament patriarchs and people of God were polygamous, and although Jesus may have proclaimed life-long monogamy to be the Christian ideal, he said nothing about the superiority of any one form of family life to all others.

Indeed, the family unit as we define it today in the West – husband, wife and children living as a self-contained domestic unit, bounded by four walls, within which mother stays at home to do the housework and rear the children and beyond which father goes to earn his own and their support – is a relatively recent phenomenon. A direct product of the Enlightenment and the Industrial Revolution, the 'modern' family began to emerge in Europe after the Renaissance and the Reformation and was probably born full-grown in the New World, due in no small way, I suspect, to Puritan influences.

In his fascinating and compelling study, *The Making of the Modern Family*, Edward Shorter pictures the family as a ship which 'in the Bad Old Days – let us say the sixteenth and seventeenth centuries' was held fast to its moorings by ties of kin, community and ancestral traditions, all of which were to be severed as it journeyed into the modern world.[8] Moreover, taking the metaphor further, he argues that it was not the strong currents of capitalism, anonymous urban life and the great tides of rationality and secularism, over which the family had no control, which caused the ship to slip its moorings and drift on the high seas, but the crew itself – Mum, Dad and the kids – who severed the cables 'by gleefully reaching down and sawing them through so that the solitary voyage could commence.' (This may be, like most bold hypotheses, an overstatement, because the context of culture and society must have had some effect on its inhabitants; nonetheless he has a point.) Shorter devotes the remainder of his book to developing his argument that a surge of sentiment in three areas helped to dislodge what he calls the 'traditional' family and replace it with the 'modern' nuclear variety. (He defines the 'traditional' family as a family which operates in a society where people are willing to put the demands of their community above their personal ambitions and desires.)

First, in the area of *courtship*, romantic love replaced material considerations in bringing the couple together. Property and lineage – concerns about inheritance, kinship and class for example – gave way to personal happiness and individual self-development as criteria for choosing a marriage partner. In rural Ireland, as I grew up, I recall sons being disinherited because their parents had eloped, marrying 'beneath them' without family approval. And in Africa I listened to young trainee teachers calculating when they would be able to afford the bridewealth in cash or kind due to the bride's father on marriage. In many societies parents still negotiate the dowry to be brought by the bride.

Second, in the *mother-child relationship*, the infant was to come to occupy centre stage. A residual affection, due to the biological link, may always have existed between mother and child but the mother in traditional society was desperately struggling for existence and had been prepared to place many considerations above the infant's welfare. In modern society, maternal love would see to it that his well-being came second to none. Both Shorter and Elisabeth Badinter, in her richly documented, exciting but also controversial *The Myth of Motherhood*, demonstrate persuasively, to my mind, the development of mother-love. This happened from the end of the eighteenth century onwards as first the middle classes and then the upper and lower classes, too, throughout Europe (well-documented for England and France, followed with a certain time lag elsewhere, moving from west to east), begin to abandon the practice of mercenary nursing.[9] Instead of sending their children away into the countryside or to the suburbs to a wet nurse immediately after birth, or hiring a wet nurse to live in, mothers began to nurse their own infants, either by dry-feeding or breast-feeding, with a consequent curtailment of their personal freedoms. Before the development of what might be called a 'cult of mother-love', women belonging to the upper classes, in order to free themselves for their social and intellectual pursuits, and women from the middle and lower classes, mainly for economic reasons, may be said to have shown an indifference towards their offspring bordering on neglect. As a result many children died. One middle-class lawyer in Vaux-le-Vicomte, France, married in 1759, exclaims how he lost all six children, and drawing up a balance sheet remarks: 'And now I find myself childless after having had six boys. Blessed be the will of God!' Similarly, the essayist Montaigne makes his famous comment on the same subject: 'I lost two or three children during their stay with the wet nurse – not without regret, mind you, but without great vexation.'[10] And what better proof of indifference than both parents' absence from the burials of their children – it was unusual for them to attend the funeral of a child under five years of age.

Third, the *boundary line between the family and the surrounding community* began to shift and was redrawn. Formerly, as Shorter so imaginatively states it, 'The family's shell was pierced full of holes, permitting people from outside to flow freely through the household, observing and monitoring. The traffic flowed the other way, too, as members of the family felt they had more in common emotionally with the various peer groups than with one another. In other words, the traditional family was much more a productive and reproductive unit than an emotional unit. It was a mechanism for transmitting property and position from generation to genera-tion. While the lineage was important, being together about the dinner table was not.'[11] How well I recall family members, servants and labourers mingling with one another, eating, working and socialising in the homestead of a rural Irish farm – relic of yester-year. But these priorities were reversed. And as the change took place, ties with the outside world were weakened while ties binding members of the family to one another were reinforced. In the words of Shorter again, 'A shield of privacy was erected to protect the foyer's intimacy from foreign intrusion. And the modern nuclear family was born in the shelter of domesticity.'[12]

Badinter goes further than Shorter, in arguing for the absence
of any such thing as the 'maternal instinct' and putting in its place,
rather convincingly, a cultivated mother-love. Moreover, mother-
love cannot be taken for granted and, already peering above the
horizon, may be its complement and successor, father-love.
'Apparently,' she observes, ' "mother love" is no longer the exclusive prerogative of women. Many present-day fathers behave like
mothers, love their children like them – blurring what was once
so obstinately viewed as a necessary distinction between paternal
and maternal love.'[13]

Space does not permit us to discuss all the forces which have
contributed to this monumental change and the sexual revolutions
of the late eighteenth century and the 1960's: Enlightenment individualism; the Industrial Revolution and consequent urbanisation
and depersonalisation; the publication of Rousseau's *Émile* in 1862,
calling for a 'return to nature';[14] the abandonment of swaddling
clothes and the return to maternal breast-feeding; the invention of
the baby bottle and sterilisation which rendered it safe; the need
for a demographic increase (in France during her wars); revivals
of religion; campaigns for social and moral reform; Freudian
psychoanalysis (which apportioned an undue proportion of blame
for all ills to deficient 'mothering'); and, most recent of all, the
invention of comparatively safe methods of contraception and
abortion.

3. Parents of the future

On closer examination things are rarely what they seem to be. And
I hope that it is clear by now that many popular assumptions
about the family, the man-woman relationship, masculinity and
femininity, and the mother-child relationship are unfounded. It is
on the basis of such a clearing away of the undergrowth that I
propose to make a series of suggestions about the future of man
and woman in the home.

If man and woman are created *persons of equal value* in the
image of God, then from the outset, from the very beginning of a
relationship, the couple meet face to face as free persons, each

with a duty to respect the other's personal integrity. There must be no question of inferiority, no sense of either being the other's property or slave, no suggestion of treating the other person as a thing – a means to any end, however noble – nothing but a full personal relationship based on genuine dialogue. Let us return to the disagreement between Marabel and Charlie Morgan about decision-making and conflicting plans. I see no reason why a couple should not openly discuss all issues concerning them both, thus eliminating the need for 'subterfuge', 'wiliness', 'deception' or 'deviousness' by either party – tactics which serve only to diminish personhood and stunt real personal growth.

If man and woman are created *male and female* in the image of God, then from the outset the couple also meet face to face as sexual beings with different reproductive functions and certain distinctive characteristics, perhaps complementary, as yet not fully understood and mysterious in nature and origin. Each must give to the other his or her conjugal rights in an attitude of mutual submissiveness. A remark was made to me a short time ago about the marriage relationship accentuating the man's 'masculinity' and the woman's 'femininity'. This may indeed be so, but who has decided what is essentially masculine and feminine and has the environment, as well as heredity, played a part in developing the role stereotypes? It seems to me that wholeness will be revealed only by a positive affirmation of sex and the exploration of all that mutual submissiveness entails, not by relating on the basis of stereotyped characteristics such as 'masculine aggressiveness' and 'feminine passivity'.

If man and woman are created in the image of God *for relationship*, to become one flesh, then in true companionate marriage each of the partners must forsake all other competing ties and allow for the full development of the other's potential as a person and as a spouse. For example, if a man and woman are educated and professionally trained, each in his or her own sphere, whether or not they have pursued a career before marriage, each must recognise the need for the other to develop both gifts and potential. Moreover, on the one hand, neither spouse's family nor friends, work nor play nor indeed any emotional need, real or imagined, must be allowed to prevent the couple from growing together into unity. On the other hand, hedging about the home, making it into a secure 'nest of domestic bliss' into which to retreat, will rarely ensure long-term success. What is needed is rather the development of a mature relationship in interaction with the community outside.

If man and woman are commanded *to be fruitful in procreation* then they must be prepared as parents to take some responsibility for nurturing the new life created. So long as the nuclear family remains the basic unit of society and the place where the men and women of future generations spend their formative years, then an increasing divorce rate will pose a threat to the growth of stable personalities and the future of society. In the past the procreative function of the marriage relationship was over-stressed; nowadays, it is the attachment arising out of romantic love and the glorification of sex which is in danger of tipping the balance. Until and unless society as a whole provides a better and healthier way of rearing its children then intending parents must take their responsibility seriously under God.

If man and woman are commanded *to rule the earth and subdue it,* to have dominion as stewards of God over the rest of creation, then they must be prepared to work together, each playing his or her part in joint responsibility. For instance, if a woman is endowed with creative and artistic talents should she not use them for the benefit of humankind, rather than hiding them just because she is the one who carries the couple's child? Did Jesus' parable of the talents apply only to men (Matt. 25.14–30)?

Given these propositions and the fact that the family is a social institution and many, if not all, sex roles are interchangeable, then it seems to me that great possibilities lie ahead for men and women as parents.

Considering, for example, the realities of post-industrial society and the implications of the technological and cybernetics revolutions, why should not each couple decide who ought to go out to work, so to speak – although this too may change in the computer age? And should they not share all tasks equally, or, at least according to agreed proportions and divisions of labour? There seem to be no good reasons why adjustments at home and at work cannot be made. Many of the contested issues are still unresolved both in scientific and sociological terms. For instance, the age at which a child may be weaned continues to be debated, some researchers putting it at between six and eight weeks, others at five months or more. Again, why should not more fathers, if they so wish, cultivate 'mother love' and be involved in the early years of a child's development? What fate, then, 'masculine' rationality and aggressiveness and 'feminine' emotionality and sensitivity? At present, the pressures put on an isolated housewife and mother who is denied the outlet of wider social intercourse, frequently lead to depression, and the pressures placed on an overworked husband by an overly competitive and aggressive market place often contribute to heart attacks. Some form of work-sharing, therefore, would appear not only possible but highly desirable and full of hope for a better future.

However, not only the traditionalists but also the psychoanalysts, fearing a paradise lost, express grave reservations about the kind of proposals which I have just made. Why? The main cause for disquiet centres round the interchangeability of roles which work-sharing seems to require. A child's sexual identity, they feel, is threatened because of the blending of roles and the consequent blurring of distinctions. But I would hazard a guess that some of the fears are unfounded: from an anthropological standpoint roles vary a great deal from one society to another; it is stability within a system which counts.[15] I suspect that psychoanalysts may in fact be confusing sex distinctions with role differentiation which I believe are related but not necessarily identical. There is no evidence to suggest that interchangeability of certain roles and functions will lead to the much feared unisexism or contribute to the development of androgynous beings. On the basis of our present state of knowledge it is equally, if not more likely, that partnership between men and women will open up a whole new dimension of human potentiality. Then we shall truly know what it is really like to be man or woman, male or female, masculine or feminine, bisexual beings created in the image of God, re-created and united in Christ, and intended for relationship one with the other. It will be paradise regained.

> When Adam delved and Eve
>   span
> Woman, no doubt, was less
>   than man.
> When Eve begins to delve as
>   well,
> How can folks Eve from
>   Adam tell?
> So Adam must his pride
>   maintain
> By boasting a superior brain.
> But this false claim is
>   knocked for six
> When Eve goes into politics.
> So what is left for Adam still
> Except to steal and rape and
>   kill?
> Unless you think – and
>   you'd be right –
> That Eve and Adam in God's
>   sight
> Are equal partners in the
>   strife
> Of building up the common life.
>
>   Rupert Davies[16]

Conclusions

That there were two distinct Martha traditions only goes to show that what we think is a modern phenomenon or problem is probably as old as the human race. However, for the first time in history we have the knowledge and the resources, both material and spiritual, to allow for either role or a combination of both at the same time. Man and woman separately and together in the home are Martha's true heirs of the future. 'A good marriage is a life,' said Archbishop Robert Runcie to Prince Charles and Lady Diana Spencer at their wedding in St Paul's Cathedral, in July 1981, quoting the poet, Edwin Muir; it is:

Where each asks from each
What each most wants to give
And each awakes in each
What else would never be.[17]

8: Stewards of God
Women at work

'When I ask you to earn money and have a room of your own,
I am asking you to live in the presence of reality. . . .'
Virginia Woolf[1]

The Priestly creation narrative (Gen. 1.1–2.4a) makes a fundamental distinction between the blessing which God confers on Man
and that which he confers on the birds of the air and the creatures
of the sea. Both are told to be fruitful and multiply but Man alone,
as male and female, created in the image and likeness of God, is
told not only to fill the earth but 'to subdue it; and have dominion
over the fish of the sea and over the birds of the air and over every
living thing that moves upon the earth' (Gen. 1.22, 26–8).

For present purposes two things should be noted in this account.
First, it is generic Man, man as male and female, who is entrusted
with lordship over creation, especially over the animals. Second,
it is Man made in the image and likeness of God who is given this
task; he becomes God's steward, an intermediary between the
Creator and the rest of creation.[2] Note also, incidentally, that men
are not given authority to lord it over one another; so often in the
history of the people of God Man has usurped God's authority in
relation to his fellows and pillaged and raped the earth despite his
stewardship. To neglect the ecological concerns of today's world
and to abandon planet earth to possible nuclear destruction is not
taking stewardship seriously. And man and woman, Christian and
non-Christian alike, are equally responsible – but especially Christians, as Scripture makes so abundantly clear.

Jesus' parable of the talents is related (with certain modifications)
by Matthew, first of the four Evangelists, in a chapter where he

brings together a number of parables of the kingdom. The kingdom of heaven is likened to a certain man going on a journey who calls his servants and entrusts them with his property. To one he gives five talents, to another two, to a third one, each according to his ability. We are then told how on his return the master finds that the first two have doubled the value of their talents while the third has buried his in the ground for safe-keeping. The first two are commended for their goodness and faithfulness and the third is condemned for his wickedness and laziness (Matt. 25.14–30).

The parable's meaning and that of its nearest parallel, the parable of the pounds as recorded by Luke (Luke 19.11–27), is much debated.[3] But, at the very least, we can claim that Jesus expects responsible and faithful use of what he has entrusted to his people. In Jesus' time the Jews and their leaders, who had been entrusted with proclaiming God's rule, were failing in their responsibility. Today, we too, men and women belonging to the people of God, as stewards of his grace, are entrusted not only with the message of God's kingdom, but also with the carrying out of its mandate. Traditionally, the Protestant work ethic has been seen as part of that mandate, a dutiful exercising of our stewardship. But it has lacked wholeness, often neglecting ecological factors and almost totally excluding women from the area of dominion. Like the Jews we, too, are failing in our responsibility. The time has come for women not to evade their responsibility, not to waste their energies and gifts, but instead to take their place alongside men as stewards of God in the world.

1. Why not work?

To be a housewife in the towns and villages of medieval Britain meant something quite different from what it means to be a house-wife today. Then, prior to the changes which were to result from the Reformation, the English Revolution (and Puritanism) and the Industrial Revolution, the family was a self-contained economic unit and the home had not yet been separated from the productive and industrial spheres. In village and in town women were linked to production, not just vicariously through their husbands, but directly, as an integral part of an economic enterprise. Domestic or woman's work – housework – had therefore a much wider definition than it does today.

In the villages, women took part in milling, brewing, baking, dairying, the care of poultry and the rearing of pigs, the growing of fruit and vegetables, the spinning of flax and wool as well as in nursing and doctoring. True, these areas were often designated specifically 'woman's work' but the lines were much more loosely drawn than, for example, those which would later define the rigid division of labour characteristic of the industrial era. Moreover, when there was a surplus of women in the household, woman's work extended to ploughing the fields and harvesting the crops. As I have already said, in my childhood in rural Ireland I recall seeing women managing large households, milking the cows, separating the milk, feeding the animals and at times driving tractors and forking hay.

In the towns, there were few guilds from which women were explicitly excluded. Records reveal that they worked as barbers, furriers, carpenters, saddlers, joiners and in numerous other trades. Every female member of a merchant's household would engage in some form of economic activity. And many of these women supervised large households, delegating the duties in order to free themselves to engage in mercantile activities.

In all such households, in town and country, as I have witnessed in contemporary Africa, children grew up in an open environment, in the context of a large household and a busy working community. They were never 'tied to their mother's apron strings', so to speak, but entertained at work and play by grandparents, older brothers and sisters, aunts and uncles, hired nurses and servants and, in the towns, by apprentices as well.[4]

Yet, as we have already seen in the last chapter, a great number of forces conspired to make industrial and capitalist society abandon the 'traditional' or extended family for the 'modern' or nuclear family and initiate a cult of mother love. The new climate of opinion so exalted motherhood and infant care as the true calling of every woman, the manifestation of the truly feminine, that first the middle classes, then the aristocracy and lower classes withdrew into domestic solitude and cosiness. Only the working classes, out of sheer economic necessity and because they were the sources of cheap labour in the new market place of industrial society, allowed their women to work outside the home.

True, even in medieval times, the ideologies of church and state affirmed the dominance of the male in the ecclesiastical and political spheres, but it was the exclusion of woman from the productive (social and economic) sphere and her banishment into the confined space of the nuclear household, her chaining to the hearth as wife and mother alone, which signalled her final enslavement and almost simultaneously gave rise to the demands for woman's emancipation.

Why not work? Because the wife of a prosperous or well-bred man did not need to work in gainful employment outside the home. The mark of a lady was to be accomplished in the genteel arts of music, painting and embroidery. The mark of a true mother was to be responsible for feeding and bringing up her own children, if not literally, then at least in a supervisory capacity. And Christians complied: this was not only the truly feminine but also the truly Christian calling of woman. To this day, as a result, feelings of fear and guilt engulf women who contemplate leaving their young children for the school or the market place.

2. Why work?

Unmarried women and widows, divorcees and single parents go out to work as a matter of course to earn a living, but not so married women, especially if they have young children. For although between 1931 and 1970 the number of 'economically active' women in Britain increased by 45 per cent so that by 1980 there were approximately 10.4 million women and 15.6 million men in the labour force, the question as to whether married women with families should go out to work still arouses controversy.[5]

Married women enter into gainful employment, admittedly, for a variety of reasons, the most common being because of economic factors, a desire for independence, a means of being useful and fulfilled, out of boredom and feelings of 'emptiness', and from habit.

The most obvious reason – to acquire more money – has itself several motivating forces: to survive; to eat better and dress well; to maintain living standards – such as keeping up the mortgage repayments – in the face of inflation; to run a second car; to buy a holiday cottage; to provide for a child's private education and so we might go on. Who works for survival, you may ask? Well, there are many families in Britain in which the wife is the main breadwinner and others where the husband is so poorly paid that the family needs his wife's wage. The last census of England and Wales revealed a total of 267,470 families, or 2 per cent of all married families, in which the wife was the main breadwinner – and this figure does not include the unemployed, only those whose husbands were in part-time work or who were economically inactive. Other families, such as those where the husband works in the lower-paid echelons of the National Health Service, also need the supplementary wage which the wife brings home. Of course there does come a point when the distinction must be made between necessity and luxury; it is irrelevant, however, for present purposes.

A woman's desire for independence, self-esteem, the feeling of being human, belongingness – call it what you will – is closely related to the economic reasons for working, as it usually involves the need for a niche of one's own and the wish not to have to rely on another for a 'handout', however freely given: to have money and a room of one's own.

Also, closely related to the desire for independence and belongingness is the wish, especially in the skilled and professional woman, to do a useful piece of work, of value to the wider world outside the family, and the attendant need for a sense of identity and fulfilment. Moreover, sheer habit may drive the woman who has had a career before marriage – the woman who was a worker before she was a mother – back to the work place.

Yet, just as significant as any of the foregoing, and probably a key factor in any combination of reasons, is the relentless boredom and emptiness of the domestic treadmill, especially when the children have left home for school or work and overworked father is still at the office. For many women home has become a surburban prison from which to escape in all haste. When *Woman's Own* magazine conducted a survey into working mothers they found that over half worked because they were lonely and bored at home, and desperately needed a break. Asked if they would still go out to work even if they had no need of the money, four out of five answered in the affirmative.[6] Recently, a mother of five, all now at school or university, vacating one job and contemplating another, told me how she would be bored and wasted without a new job because she had learnt to do the essential housework in a day. So much for full-time motherhood in the age of domestic appliances and convenience foods.

3. What kind of work?

Not only are women servants in the home but the vast majority of women who go out to work are employed in what are called the service industries and in semi-skilled or unskilled jobs. As claimed by the Equal Opportunities Commission in 1980, there may have been a breakthrough for a minority of women who became blacksmiths, dockers, motor mechanics, metal brokers, bricklayers, pilots or entered a variety of other spheres normally reserved for men. Yet, neither the ten-year campaign waged by women's liberationists nor the passing of the Sex Discrimination Act stopped the process by which women in Britain were steadily eased out of skilled jobs in the course of this century. Between 1911 and 1971 women's share of skilled (higher-paid) manual work dropped by almost *half*, from 24 per cent to 13.5 per cent, while their share of unskilled manual jobs more than *doubled*, from 15.5 per cent to 37.2 per cent. This astonishing trend, amounting to a 'breakthrough' of men into a near-monopoly of skilled work continued during the seventies. Similarly, neither the trade unions' pledge to fight for equal pay nor the Equal Pay Act itself achieved any real 'breakthrough' for women. Women's pay has been held down with such remarkable tenacity that by the end of the seventies women at work were still taking home 36 per cent less money than their male counterparts. In 1979, for example, for every pound in the average man's pay packet there was only 63.6 pence in the average woman's. Or, to make the same point in another way, in 1970, a man earned on average £29.70 per week and a woman £16.20, a differential of £13.50 (a woman's weekly wage thus being 54.5 per cent of a man's); in 1979, a man earned on average £99.00 per week and a woman £63.00, a differential of £36.00 (a woman's weekly wage thus being 63.6 per cent of a man's). In other words, there has been an improvement of only 9.1 per cent in ten years, five of these under the new Act.

One can well imagine the implications for one-parent families and the family where the woman is the main breadwinner. But the arguments used by employers and trade unionists alike to justify this kind of inequality are based on the concept of the *family wage* which assumes the man to be the main breadwinner. Take, for example, the statement of a male delegate to the Civil Service Clerical Association in 1966: 'What we want is to give breadwinners throughout the country enough pay to keep their wives at home.'[8] A nice sentiment, perhaps, but I wonder if he consulted his wife. The concept of the family wage is an anachronism in our post-industrial, technological society with its changing family structures and fast-developing patterns of employment. What price the microchip? The question is seldom asked and even more rarely understood.

More specifically, what kinds of jobs do women do? As already noted, women are employed overwhelmingly in the service industries (industries which do not produce goods and which involve personal service) such as banking, insurance, hairdressing, cleaning and all sorts of public administrative work like teaching, nursing, social and secretarial work. Between 1961 and 1980 more than two million women joined the service industries while at the same time half a million left the productive industries. As a result, by the early eighties, more than three-quarters of all women at work were in the non-productive sector which means the lower-status, lower-paid sector. And even as men have monopolised skilled manual work they have continued to get more than their fair share of the prestigious and highly paid jobs in other areas too. For instance, over the course of several years women non-manual workers have increased their share of managerial and administrative jobs by a tiny margin – from 19.8 per cent to 21.6 per cent – but at the same time they have more than tripled their share of clerical work – from 21.4 per cent to 73.2 per cent. And jobs which at the beginning of the century had a fair balance between the sexes were transformed by the seventies into 'typically feminine' forms of employment. For example, ninety-nine per cent of all typists, shorthand writers and secretaries are women, but only 14 per cent of office managers. Moreover, microchip technology is not improving matters as the work-force is depleted and former secretaries, used to performing skilled tasks such as high-speed shorthand typing and personal services about the office, become mere machine operators. The word-processor in the office, like the machine in the factory, will serve only to dehumanise and alienate its operators. Similarly, the teaching profession, once a largely female profession, shows a familiar pattern. Eighty-nine per cent of infant and primary-school teachers are female. Male teachers predominate in secondary schools and in senior posts, more often than not teaching mathematics, science and other supposedly 'masculine' subjects. In 1976 women accounted for 59.3 per cent of the full-time teaching force, yet filled only 38.4 per cent of the headships. The change to comprehensive and co-educational schools has meant that women have fewer opportunities for promotion to top jobs. In fact, more than three-quarters of all female teachers are in the lower-paid jobs (scales 1 and 2) compared with less than half of all males.[9]

Another interesting and significant development that took place as the balance of types of work shifted was the segregation of men and women in the work place. Men and women began to be concentrated in separate areas until there was a staggering degree of total segregation, so that men and women end up doing jobs where no member of the opposite sex does the same thing at the same place. A 1980 study revealed that 45 per cent of women and about 75 per cent of men work in totally segregated jobs. In other words, in the course of the present century, the likelihood of men working in an all-male environment has increased considerably.

A complex network of social and political factors have no doubt led to the situation just described. Probably of greatest significance is the fact that in a male-dominated society men hold the reins of power and use it to secure the prestigious and, therefore, the more highly paid jobs for themselves. Of course, rigid role-stereotyping and strict division of labour contribute to, and, it would appear, over a period of time, reinforce the existing patterns. Consequently, whatever law is enacted, no real change will take place until the power-structures are overturned and women have at least some, if not equal, say in the matter.

4. Ought women to work?

There are, I believe, good theological, psychological, sociological and philosophical arguments for why a woman should work outside the four walls of the modern home, at least for a substantial period of her married life. The final decision, of course, must rest with the woman and her husband.

First, it can be argued, as I have done in the introduction to this chapter, that woman as well as man is given dominion over creation and authority to subdue the earth. Woman, every bit as much as man, is a steward of God and recipient of his gifts and ought not to evade her responsibility or waste the resources with which she has been endowed by her Creator, the more so if the sexes are believed to be complementary to each other.

Second, it can be argued that because the human infant needs close contact with its mother for at least the first year of its life in order to develop a whole personality, then a working mother must take a year off work after childbirth. Research also points to the child's need for close bodily contact then and later, kissing and caressing as well as breast-feeding. I have already drawn attention to differences of opinion among the experts on this subject. Yet, even if an infant can be weaned in six weeks and father-love be cultivated, let us take the one-year period as a given. Paul Tournier then suggests, in order to solve the dilemma of the working mother (and recognising a woman's peculiar contribution to the world of work), a mandatory one-year maternity leave paid for by the community or state along the same lines as retirement pensions. But he is not so naïve as not to foresee that under present working conditions mothers would be the first to resist such provision. It could lessen their chances of employment as employers have not yet come to terms with part-time jobs or the concept of work-sharing.[10] In the meantime, it is to be hoped that communities and neighbours might work out programmes and rotas to cater for the welfare of the children of working mothers in their midst. What must be avoided is the kind of arrangement which produces the so-called 'latch-key child' – the child who goes to school with the front-door key strung round his neck for safety – with all the dire consequences for personality development of which the psychiatrists warn us. But it must not be taken for granted that a non-working mother is by definition a 'better mother' – whatever that may mean – because a mother who works outside the home may be more fulfilled, less frustrated and irritable and, therefore, more relaxed and patient with her children. For other reasons, too, some psychologists argue for the desirability of woman's presence in the workaday world: every area of life will be enriched, made more whole by the contribution of woman's specifically 'feminine' gifts. Whether or not one subscribes to any theory of 'masculine' and 'feminine' distinctiveness it still holds that the contribution of both sexes should help towards the humanisation of society.

Third, it can be argued that over the centuries society has ascribed an inferior position to women as a group, similar to that ascribed to peoples of divergent race and class. And what superiors classify as inferior they tend to treat as defective or substandard in various ways. Moreover, dominant groups usually define one or two roles as acceptable for subordinates and these are generally the performing of services which they do not wish to perform themselves, for example, cleaning up the dominant group's waste products.[11] I recall, for instance, being stranded for a few days in Cairo Airport and observing with fascination how the skin colour lightened the higher up the ladder of promotion I looked, from the black man sweeping the floor to the white man sitting in the executive's chair. So, in a society where males are dominant and powerful and allocate the jobs, the service industries – and let's face it, housework is a private service industry – are largely staffed by women. Consequently, one way for woman to change the power-structures is to go out to work and begin to occupy the positions of power.

Fourth, it can be argued that woman must not acquiesce when she is told that she is doing an equally if not more valuable job in the home than men are doing outside, the two roles and the two spheres being equal but different.[12] Betty Friedan provides us with a somewhat amusing (or laughable) but typical version of this kind of reasoning. In March 1949, *Ladies' Home Journal* published a paean to the housewife from its famous columnist, Dorothy Thompson, answering the kind of woman who complains that she gets a feeling of inferiority when she has to write 'Occupation: Housewife' on the census form. The trouble with this kind of woman, Thompson scolds, is that she does not realise she is an expert in a dozen careers, simultaneously:

> You might write: business manager, cook, nurse, chauffeur, dressmaker, interior decorator, accountant, caterer, teacher, private secretary – or just put down philanthropist. . . . All your life you have been giving away your energies, your skills, your talents, your services, for love.[13]

And when she continues to complain that although she is now fifty and has not followed the career in music which she longed for in her youth she is told to consider how she is fulfilling her own ambitions in her children. Refusing to see that the woman has any case, Thompson accuses her of self-pity and exclaims, 'You are one of the most successful women I know.'

The housewife must look at things realistically, and so indeed must columnists like Dorothy Thompson. Work done within the four walls of the home is undervalued; it is done in private and therefore lacks the status accorded to work done in public. Moreover, work is rewarded according to its value and woman's work in the home goes unrewarded. It may be true that 'behind every great man there is a woman', and behind she certainly is, unrecognised and unrewarded in terms of the world's own system of values. If status-seeking is deemed inappropriate to woman why is status a measure of worth in a man's world?

The anthropologist, Margaret Mead, has remarked that in every known human society, the male's need for achievement can be recognised so that men's work is always regarded as more important than women's, whatever its nature:

> In every known human society, the male's need for achievement can be recognized. Men may cook or weave or dress dolls or hunt humming-birds, but if such activities are appropriate occupations of men, then the whole society, men and women alike, votes them as important. When the same occupations are performed by women, they are regarded as less important. In a great number of human societies men's sureness of their sex role is tied up with their right, or ability, to practise some activity that women are not allowed to practise. Their maleness, in fact, has to be underwritten by preventing women from entering some field or performing some feat. Here may be found the relationship between maleness and pride; that is, a need for prestige that will outstrip the prestige which is accorded to any woman. There seems no evidence that it is necessary for men to surpass women in any specific way, but rather that men do need to find reassurance in achievement, and because of this connexion, cultures frequently phrase achievement as something that women do not or cannot do, rather than directly as something which men do well.
>
> The recurrent problem of civilization is to define the male role satisfactorily enough. . . .[14]

Woman has always had the obvious role of childbearing while man, it can be argued, is forced to find a role. So rather than Freudian 'penis envy' among young girls who want to be boys we have instead male jealousy of woman's capacity to hold the future of the human race in her womb! A major hope for change in this state of affairs is the fact that increasingly in our modern world the time needed for childbearing and childrearing purposes is decreasing, if only for demographic reasons. In the meantime, some men may continue to feel threatened as women take up jobs hitherto regarded as male preserves. In the circumstances both parties to the conflict must display a measure of realism.

Conclusions

I conclude therefore that although there are good theological and other reasons why a married woman should engage in work other than housework, there is still a great deal of prejudice and a number of inequalities with which she will have to contend in the workplace. Prejudice against working mothers and inequalities of opportunity, status and pay must still be faced. However, given the present changes both in employment patterns and family structures, there is hope that, together, women and men will find a way forward which will contribute ultimately to a more whole way of living and working for all. For what is good for woman is good for man, at the most fundamental of levels.

9: The chosen few
Women and the single life

'What shall I do? My soul cleaves to the Law;
but others keep the world going!'
An unmarried rabbi defending himself[1]

I was taking a stroll with a friend through the fields of Nandi country in the highlands of western Kenya. The late afternoon sunshine was warm, the air crisp and at times acrid with smoke, wafting its way upwards through the thatched roofs of small homesteads dotted in clusters across the wide open marshes and grasslands. At the time I was lecturing at the nearby teachers' college and quite frequently took a walk when afternoon classes had finished. This particular afternoon we were stopped and greeted by an old woman. 'Is it well?' she enquired.

Fortunately, my friend was fluent in the local dialect, so we responded, 'Is it well, old woman?'

'Are you well?' she continued.

'Yes,' we replied.

Whereupon she proceeded in the usual Nandi manner to enquire after husband, children and livestock. Perplexity and bewilderment, however, followed the disclosure that neither of us had a husband, either in Kenya or overseas (as she had suggested). Nevertheless, she went on, undaunted, to enquire after the children. (Imagine our amazement and amusement.) But no children! This was indeed impossible, unbelievable! Yet, she had to concede eventually, apparently true enough. We then parted on the understanding that she would make appropriate and discreet arrangements for the begetting of children, husband or no! Only later was I to realise the full implications of her bewilderment and kindhearted promise: she was alluding to the practice of 'woman marriage' where a childless older woman is married to a younger woman and the services of a visiting genitor engaged to perform the role of biological father.[2]

For the old woman and her people a woman without children to continue the lineage and inherit the land was inconceivable. Imagine the disruptions to world view and social structure caused by Christian missionaries who were single and childless and had no apparent intention of ever getting married!

Ironically, however, Western culture itself and the Christian church display an ambivalence towards single people, particularly single women, which may at times include an incredulity akin to the old woman's. The single woman, especially the never-married, is at once pitied, despised and envied. Marriage is considered to be the norm: those who remain single have 'missed the boat' or been 'left on the shelf', or still 'roam free'.

1. A question of choice?

(i) The gift of celibacy

According to the teaching of Jesus as recorded in Matthew 19.1–12 neither celibacy nor marriage is commanded; either can be a state in which to serve God. The Jewish norm was marriage, and eunuchs, even more than tax-collectors, were excluded from the people of God (Deut. 23.1). Therefore Jesus, in accepting eunuchs, was being characteristically shocking and unconventional. Nevertheless, to see the meaning of celibacy, he admits, is something which must be 'given'. Here, Jesus' teaching is close to that of Paul. Paul, unlike official Judaism, placed a high value on celibacy. Yet, unlike the monks of Qumran and the later church Fathers who exalted celibacy or the virginal state, he did not rate the celibate person as spiritually superior to the married, although he stated a personal preference for the single state and wished others would follow his example. In 1 Corinthians 7.7 he clearly teaches that celibacy is a *charism*, a special gift from God to certain individuals. And although gifts do not signify 'special-service Christians', they do merit recognition within the church. In sum, according to Paul, marriage remains the norm but God may choose certain individuals and endow them with the gift of celibacy.

Commenting on the Matthean passage Eduard Schweizer summarises concisely and elegantly the New Testament teaching on the subject:

> There is thus no hint of any double moral standard. Neither is there any reference to an ideal of poverty or to the virtue of asceticism. . . . Jesus shares with his whole nation the unbroken affirmation of God's good creation, which is also the basis of marriage, even though the Kingdom of heaven, that is, the world of God to come, can cast light on celibacy. Generally, men testify their approval of God's creation by marriage and bringing up their children; some, however, are especially called to prefigure the end and goal of creation, God's new world in which men and women will not marry (22.30).[3]

Unfortunately, the majority of Christians, past and present, either ignore the teaching of the New Testament altogether and affirm marriage alone as constituting God's will for humankind or, conversely, believe that Jesus and Paul exalted the single state to a special place above the married, considering celibacy to be God's higher calling for his children.[4] To my mind, both views are wrong-headed and fly in the face of nature and grace, reason and revelation. According to the teaching of Jesus and the express opinions of Paul, some of us may be given the gift of celibacy and can therefore remain single, while others of us, who are endowed with different gifts, may lack this particular gift and are consequently well-advised to marry.[5]

(ii) Categories of singleness

There are, however, many different states of singleness. There is the kind of person alluded to already, who is called by God to the celibate life (whether for a limited time or for life) for the sake of the kingdom, and is promised grace to meet the rigours of what is not always an easy, albeit a clear and fulfilling vocation. But there is also the never-married who does not accept the single state as a vocation and longs for marriage; the widowed who once knew the love and companionship of a happy marriage and feels deeply the loss of a spouse; the divorced or single parent who smarts from the hurt of a failed relationship and anxiously faces the rearing of a family single-handed; and the homosexual who cannot marry and may, for a variety of reasons, experience deep personal guilt and social ostracism. The number of people in these categories is considerable. For example, in Britain only half the men over forty years of age are once-married with children, while in the United States 16.5 million women over the age of twenty-five are single, 4.2 million having never married and the remaining 12.3 million having ended up separated, widowed or divorced. Many of the joys, problems and dangers which singles encounter are common to all ages and categories and are experienced by men and women alike. This should be borne in mind as we turn our attention to the unmarried single woman who remains so either because of choice or circumstances, or, as is often the case, a combination of both.

2. A matter of sex

Sex today is not only an explosive but an all-pervasive subject. Advertisements, television plays, newspaper features and a constant flow of statistics concerning marriage and divorce and sexual deviancy all serve to remind us of the central part played by sex in modern Western society. A strong sexual drive is part of the human condition and the regulation of sexual relations is fundamental to any social structure. The history of civilisation is the history of sexual control and the swing of the pendulum from extreme asceticism to permissiveness and sexual license. Unfortunately, the Christian church, aided by its Greek cultural and philosophical heritage and the reactions of former libertarians and bohemians such as Augustine, has for the most part affirmed the procreative function of sexual intercourse while denouncing any pleasures associated with the sex act itself. It was only after the Renaissance and the Reformation challenge to the virginal ideal that the marriage relationship began once again to be seen as

inherently good. Even then, throughout the Victorian era and well
into the present, twentieth, century, the various Christian churches
have continued to display a somewhat ambivalent attitude towards
sex. Traditionalist Roman Catholics and certain types of fundamentalists continue to do so. For me, as for my contemporaries
and immediate predecessors, sex education and sexual ethics were
confined to exhortations about avoiding pregnancy before marriage
so as not to cause the birth of an illegitimate child. Such was the
theology of sex, love and marriage. It is little wonder that Christians found themselves at a loss as the whole scenario changed
with the flowering of romantic love and the discovery of the contraceptive pill in the mid-twentieth century.

While it is, as already argued, true that we are neither male nor
female before we are persons, it is equally certain that we are no
persons without being male or female. Sexuality is an integral part
of being human. And humans are complex wholes, comprising
body, mind and spirit, no part functioning apart from the other
except in abnormal circumstances. For this reason I find it difficult
to divorce love from sex. Consequently, in coitus two people meet
in their totality as persons so that casual, non-committed sexual
relationships cannot be other than unfulfilling, fragmenting and
ultimately destructive of the personality. It is probably for such
reasons that Paul asks rhetorically of the Corinthian Christians
'Do you not know that he who joins himself to a prostitute becomes
one body with her? For, it is written, "The two shall become
one" ' (1 Cor. 6.16). It therefore seems to me that sexual intercourse properly belongs within a committed relationship which for
Christians is normally the life-long monogamous relationship called
marriage. In such a permanent relationship love finds space to
develop and grow to maturity.[6]

The dilemma for the single Christian woman lies in how to
affirm and enjoy her sexuality outside of a marriage relationship.
Our sex-saturated, individualistic and depersonalised modern
society may add to her often acute sense of pain arising out of
sexual tension and loneliness. It is not surprising therefore that
with the increased availability and reliability of the pill some opt
for occasional experiences of genital sex within the context of close

friendship. Neither partner, it is argued, may desire marriage for a whole host of reasons and yet may wish to give and receive love.[7] And love, freely given and freely received, is required in order to live life to the full. My reservations about this approach are twofold. First, and most important, the liaison lacks the secure context of commitment necessary for the mature growth of love. Second, the unwillingness to make a commitment to permanency smacks of 'selfishness', of 'having one's cake and eating it'. Nevertheless, I am not my sister's keeper and must refrain from judging others.[8] At another level, the risks of venereal disease need to be taken into account. All that said, however, there remains much light to be shed on the subject by theologians, sociologists and psychologists alike.

3. An imperative of love

For a number of years psychologists have been drawing our attention to the importance of touch (which spells warmth, security and love) for the development of personality from very early childhood through adolescence and into adulthood. Those who, for whatever reasons, are deprived of the physical expression of love at significant stages of their development become inadequate persons in one way or another. The average single person is as much in need of touch as anybody else. And where damage has been done to the personality touch may be an aid in the healing process. This was not properly recognised in the past and people's stances on the issue varied from total denial of physical contact with other humans, through an oftentimes inordinate fondness of animals to the religious ecstasies experienced by some of the great mystics who became 'the brides of Christ'. Today, we are much more likely to recognise the need for touch – it has been called 'skin-hunger' – for what it is. The crucial question for the 'sexual celibate', then, becomes how to express love within the context of an intimate relationship without proceeding to sexual intercourse or engaging in genital sex of any kind. In most instances sexual feelings will be aroused. They must be affirmed as natural and good and not allowed to lead to feelings of guilt, and be subsequently brought under discipline and control. For many, the kiss, hug or back-rub from a friend is preferable to being deprived of the healing properties of human touch.

This is not to say that for some people sexual tension will not remain a stubborn problem. Current evidence suggests that relief is often sought and found in masturbation. Until comparatively recently masturbation was judged sinful by the church and harmful by the medical profession. Nowadays, doctors and many pastors regard the practice as a normal part of growing up for adolescents and as a legitimate means of releasing tension for others. Only when obsessive and linked to unhealthy fantasising is it destructive. For the sexual celibate, therefore, it may well provide occasional relief from a build-up of sexual tension without the risk of exploiting another.[9]

The imperative of love requires that single Christians as much as their married brothers and sisters love their fellows as Christ loved them and as they love themselves. Man, as we have already argued, is made for relationship – with God and with his fellow human beings. But the latter cannot refer exclusively to the sexual relationship between spouses, because for reasons of statistics alone not every person can marry, that is, not unless one explores patterns of marriage other than life-long monogamy between one man and one woman. If Christians are not prepared to countenance such arrangements then, in order to carry out the imperative of love, they have no choice but to develop loving relationships between singles and marrieds, across all the boundaries.

4. The problems of singleness

In a society where marriage is the norm, the problems of singleness are numerous. And most depressing is the fact that married couples, both inside and outside the church, not only fail to understand the nature of the problems when they meet them but, except for rare instances, go through life totally unaware that they exist.

We have already looked at the need to give and receive love, often most acute for the woman who has not consciously chosen to remain unmarried and who is still grappling with her plight.

Whether or not she believes celibacy to be a gift to her from God, the woman who has made a conscious choice to be single enjoys enormous advantages over her reluctantly or rebelliously unmarried sister who has to come to terms with that deep-seated feeling of rejection experienced by women who have never 'managed to catch a man'. I recall a friend admitting, 'If only I had been asked – even once', while I listened with a mixture of pity and despair. Such a woman, although encountering the same kind of problems as her consciously celibate sister, will not be able to accept them with the other's resilience or face them as a challenge; instead, she will allow each to remind her bitterly of her lonely isolation.

Recently I changed my job and moved house: indeed, I am presently suffering from the after-effects – disorientation in a new working environment, aching joints and tired muscles. But it has been fascinating to reflect on people's attitudes to a single working woman's move. There were those who never gave a thought to what it means to move house and job at the same time without the companionship or physical support of another, particularly a strong male other! There were those who obviously observed and comprehended but to whom it never occurred to lend a hand. And finally there were those local church people who happened to live nearby and who welcomed me to church and neighbourhood by putting up curtains for the first night, providing meals during the initial chaos and making themselves generally available whenever a second pair of hands was absolutely necessary. It has been a great joy to receive help so freely and willingly given. And the means of saying 'thank you' have not been difficult to find.

However, before the single woman can even think of 'moving in' she is often forced to fight a battle for the right to have a home. Thankfully, I note that my younger married friends recognise much more readily than past generations did that everybody needs a place or home of her own.[10]

Another major problem which faces the single woman especially is how to lead or regulate a necessary and fulfilling social life. She will, of course, have single friends with whom she can share outings, holidays and hobbies. But every single person should also have a number of married friends, for the benefit of all concerned.

I recall once belonging to a church where single women were used as baby-sitters. I have no objection to baby-sitting: it can be a positive way for singles to share their freedom with marrieds while becoming well-loved 'aunties' and 'uncles' to the children. But in this particular instance I noted that singles were never included in any of the family activities and were excluded from the general socialising which featured prominently among the couples. I believe every one of us was the poorer as a result. Friendship between singles and married couples can be very enriching. The mother of young children will gain immeasurably from the different perspectives and wider experience of a working woman, for example, while the single person will likewise profit from the warmth of a loving home environment and the fullness of family life. Children will benefit from days at the zoo, visits to the cinema and the pursuit of hobbies and activities with someone from outside the immediate family. And many parents like their children to have other adults available to share the joys and pains of growing up.

Of equal concern for the single woman is how she relates to people in the sphere of work and professional relations. For the most part 'sexual harassment' as an issue is a non-starter: it is deemed either to be a fiction of feminist propaganda or accepted as part of the normal scene. To my mind, the issue is much more subtle and complicated. As well as holding down a job the single working woman has to run a home and perhaps look after elderly relatives. Yet, I have known instances where the wives of colleagues have expected singles to do all the extras 'because they have all the time in the world, nothing else to do'. It is therefore with affection that I recall the jocular remark of a colleague during a time of particular pressure: 'What you need is a wife!' Moreover, I have discovered that many men do not know how to relate to a woman as a colleague, an equal: unconsciously she takes on for him the role either of a wife or a secretary (the 'office wife'). Similarly, at times I have found professional relationships severely hampered, as so many men expect any developing friendship or companionable, stimulating relationship to lead inevitably to sexual involvement, especially if the wine has been flowing freely. The price many women have to pay is constant frustration or restricted activities and increasing isolation.

It may come as a surprise to many that it is in the church, the community of faith which is the people of God, that single people, women especially, experience the most acute pain. In many churches, particularly within the evangelical tradition, the central worship event of the week is a 'family service', sometimes little more than over-age, over-size Sunday school. Similarly, the main church organisations usually cater for 'wives', 'mothers', 'couples', 'children', 'the under-thirty-fives' and 'the elderly'! What of the rest! Two of the most welcome recent developments in church life so far as singles are concerned are house groups and the weekly parish eucharist, both of which embrace a cross-section of church life, focussing on no particular age-group and thus catering for the whole family of God in that place.

5. Dangers of the single life

Needless to say, the single life is fraught with many dangers, dangers to the self and dangers within the context of relationships.

Most fundamental is the tendency to self-centredness, rigidity, perfectionism, or what is generally known as 'fussiness'. One of the obvious antidotes is to join a community or a commune, or to share a house or a flat. A more recent development has been the growth of what could be called 'scattered communities', religious orders whose members live in the midst of the wider community, alone, in pairs or in groups and provide opportunities for sharing and caring. But such ventures are not for everyone and there remains the joy of extending and receiving hospitality – one very good reason why a single person needs a home, not just 'a room of one's own' but a spare room too.

Perhaps of more common concern are the dangers which can arise from triangular relationships and exclusive friendships. In the triangular relationship, a big responsibility rests on the single person if she relates more closely to one of the partners. I recall several instances from my own past, one of which still stands out vividly. The husband and I had areas of interest in common not shared by his wife. We moved easily in and out of each other's homes and then increasingly he began calling round on his own. The red light flashed for me as my thoughts turned to his wife. It took very little imagination and ingenuity to step up my visits and so pre-empt the calls. I do not mean that I sensed anything other than genuine friendship but misunderstandings can so easily arise that it is far better to be wise before the event.

Same-sex relationships need to be handled with no less care. For some reason the end of the Victorian era saw the development of a suspicious and hostile attitude to close friendships between members of the same sex, an attitude which has persisted well into the latter half of the twentieth century. Such attitudes have not always obtained in this country and are happily now on the decline once again. Literary history is strewn with the names of those who enjoyed deep and lasting friendships. I recall with a mixture of anger and disdain the occasion overseas when I was questioned by a senior missionary about two friends who appeared to live and work very happily together. Perhaps they were not good for each other, he suggested, and ought to be separated on their return from leave. I considered the idea preposterous as so much missionary work was suffering from awkward triangular relationships and pairings of people who were totally incompatible. Why separate friends whose work was flourishing? Moreover, their home was a welcome haven for me, always a good test when exclusivism is the real danger. Every person, married or single, needs to give and receive love in the context of an intimate relationship. One of the most persistent dangers faced by the single person is the lack of perspective which may result from not being able to share life's ups and downs at the end of the day.[11] For the majority, therefore, whatever the dangers, the best solution available is to share. This is the only way of preventing aloneness from deteriorating into loneliness, solitariness and destructive withdrawal from the world.

6. Enjoying being single

All this said, the joys of the single life are deep and plentiful. The greatest bonus of all is freedom: freedom to be with others of one's choosing; freedom to be alone in solitude; freedom to be mobile, changing job and home and hobby without having to consider too many 'others'. I was reminded just a couple of weeks ago of the blessedness of my freedom when married friends with two small children who had moved house three months before me remarked how quickly I had been able to set things in order. There is also the freedom to make decisions for oneself, to buy a little luxury, perhaps, without having to consider the next pair of shoes for the children. There is also the joy of being free to have many and varied friends and being able to adjust one's plans to suit others. Contrary to popular belief single women, second only to married men (bachelors and married women fare less well), live healthy and happy lives. Statistics show that single women live more contented lives than their married sisters: a greater proportion of married women commit acts of suicide and homicide.[12]

Conclusions

God's children may be married or single. Neither state is superior to the other in terms of spiritual worth. Since, however, we are created as sexual beings, and to desire marriage is normal, God extends to his single children a special gift to live the celibate life. The deployment of this gift does not diminish a person's sexuality but rather frees the celibate to give and receive love within a secure framework of acceptance of self and others, but without recourse to genital expression. Only when the family of God's children recognises that it is made up of marrieds and singles – singles by right of choice and not by default – will singles be able to feel accepted and whole in a society both bemused and confused by sex.

10: Servants of Christ
Women in Christian Ministry

Methought that in a solemn church I stood.
Its marble acres, worn with knees and feet,
Lay spread from door to door, from street to street.
Midway the form hung high upon the rood
Of Him who gave His life to be our good;
Beyond, priests flitted, bowed, and murmured meet,
Among the candles shining still and sweet.
Men came and went, and worshipped as they could –
And still their dust a woman with her broom,
Bowed to her work, kept sweeping to the door.
Then saw I, slow through all the pillared gloom,
Across the church a silent figure come:
'Daughter,' it said, 'thou sweepest well My floor!'
'It is the Lord!' I cried, and saw no more.[1]

George Macdonald

In a recent survey on the place of women in the church carried out by the evangelical magazine, *Family*, sick-visiting came top of the 'comfort-table' – a table devised to indicate how comfortable people felt about women doing certain jobs in church.

The five hundred respondents were churchpeople of the younger generations, the two largest groups of 39 per cent and 32 per cent belonging to the twenty-five to thirty-four and thirty-five to forty-four age brackets, respectively. Of those who replied 39 per cent were men, 18 per cent were women who went out to work full-time and 43 per cent were women based at home.

After sick-visiting came counselling, helping in the Sunday school and even decorating the vicarage, while right at the bottom of the table came chairing meetings, baptising, marrying and offici-ating at funerals. Anything involving 'control' or 'ultimate authority' was rejected, while more than half said they would feel unhappy about a woman in a teaching ministry, especially one who preached when a man was available and more than four in ten thought it wrong for women to be ordained or to lead services, chair church meetings, administer communion or conduct baptisms, weddings and funerals.[2]

All this goes to show that the association of women with the so-called 'serving', 'caring' or 'helping' ministries in the church dies hard, and that evangelicals continue to be preoccupied with the relationship between women's ministry and the question of authority. No doubt a similar Catholic survey would reveal a preoccupation with the relationship between women's ministry and the question of priesthood. Evangelicals, as I have often remarked, protect the pulpit and Catholics the altar from women, as these reflect their distinctive emphases on word and sacrament. Both the 'holy' place and the place of 'power' must be defended at all costs against the onslaughts of the female hordes and so remain a male preserve.

In the foregoing chapters much has been said in support of a full ministry for women in the church. It remains to say something about Christian ministry as servanthood both for women and men and to consider briefly the main Catholic and evangelical arguments against the ordination of women.

1. Servanthood

When, during the temptations, Satan takes Jesus to a high mountain, shows him all the kingdoms of the world in their splendour and promises them to him if he will fall at his feet and worship him, Jesus replies by telling him to be off, because Scripture says that he must worship the Lord his God, and serve (*latreuseis*) him alone (Matt. 4.8–10).

When the mother of James and John, Zebedee's sons, comes with them to Jesus, requesting that they sit one on his right hand and the other on his left in his kingdom, Jesus replies that the positions are not his to give and, moreover, anyone who would be great among his disciples must be his *servant* (*diakonos*) and anyone who would be first must be a *slave* (*doulos*), just as 'the Son of Man came not to be served but to serve, and to give his life as a ransom for many' (Matt. 20.20–28).

When Paul commends himself to the Corinthian Christians it is as an apostle of Christ Jesus the Lord, one who is called to be their *servant* (*doulos*) for Jesus' sake (2 Cor. 4.5) and who proves himself God's *servant* (*diakonos*) in times of suffering (2 Cor. 6.4).

Three different Greek verbs are used, all of which signify that among his disciples Jesus expected the world's power structures to be turned upside down.[3] Alas for the church which applies his precepts only to women!

The verb *latreuein*, 'to serve', although originally used among the Greeks with the meaning 'to serve for wages or reward', came in time to signify service without any idea of pay. In the Greek version of the Old Testament, the Septuagint, it then took on religious significance, meaning 'to serve or worship cultically, especially by sacrifice'. Israel is continually to offer worship – service – not to other gods, but to Yahweh, the Lord, alone. Moreover, although the primary reference of the term is to cultic worship, such worship is only the outward expression of an inner attitude, of confident commitment to Yahweh, of a right disposition of the heart. And it is not only demanded of the priests, but of the whole people of God. This is developed in the New Testament where, except in the letter to the Hebrews, the cultic element becomes secondary and gives way to a ministry of prayer. The Christian's whole life is brought under the concept of 'service': a life of service is a life of worship. Thus Paul can call his missionary work an act of religious service, of worship of God.

The verb *diakonein*, 'to serve', as distinct from the other two words, has the special quality of indicating in very personal terms the service rendered another. It began its life in secular Greek with the meaning 'to wait on table', hence the meaning 'to provide or care for' and later 'to serve'. Among the Greeks this kind of service was not considered very dignified: ruling and not serving was proper to a man, an attitude well-expressed in the saying, 'How can a man be happy when he has to serve someone?' In Judaism, however, a deeper understanding of service began to grow and the relationship of master to servant came to be accepted, as the idea of loving one's neighbour as oneself emerged. Even so, by the time of Jesus this concept was undergoing dilution – one must not serve the unworthy – so that it had to be recovered. Jesus did so by linking, probably for the first time, the love of God and neighbour in the great new commandment, 'You shall love the Lord your God . . . and your neighbour as yourself', and by reversing the 'natural' order by declaring, 'Rather must the greatest among you become as the youngest and the leader as one who serves' (Luke 10.25–8; 22.26). Active love for the neighbour (which may include 'the enemy') becomes a mark of Christian discipleship and service the only way to greatness.

The verb *douleuein*, 'to serve', signifies slavery. Among the Greeks any type of service bearing the slightest resemblance to 'slavery' was scorned. Its mark was to let an alien will take precedence over one's own. But in the Septuagint 'to be enslaved' is used in the context of commitment to the Godhead. Usage of the verb must specify to whom the service is rendered. And in the New Testament Jesus employs the verb when he wishes to emphasise the unconditional nature of human responsibility to God. A person's own will or initiative has no place alongside the will and commission of the master, who is the Lord. The New Testament emphasis implies obedience to the will of another. Jesus Christ, Son of God, is the 'servant' par excellence: he emptied himself, taking the form of a servant (*doulos*), being born in the likeness of men (Phil. 2.7). So, too, Paul, arraigned and misunderstood by the Corinthians, became their servant (*doulos*) for Jesus' sake, literally, became a slave because of Jesus. Says Ronald Ward in commenting on the force of the word 'because' (the Greek preposition *dia* with the accusative) in this passage:

Jesus is the 'cause' of this remoter effect: Christian service. The fact of Christ induced him [Paul] to serve. We may surmise that he felt the impact of His example (John 13:5; Luke 22:26–27; cf. Gal. 5:13); was bound by His commandment (John 13:14–17); and was moved by the needs of pastoral care (1 Pet. 5:2–3).[4]

So too are all Christian disciples called to servanthood for Jesus' sake.

2. Priesthood

In an essay entitled 'Some Basic Considerations', in the symposium on *Man, Woman, and Priesthood* edited by Peter Moore, E. L. Mascall takes as his starting-point when arguing for a male priesthood that 'in the strict and proper sense, the only ontologically original and ultimate priesthood is that of Christ; it is identical with his status as Son, Word, and Apostle of the eternal Father.'[5] This priesthood, he continues, 'belongs to Christ as the *Son* of the eternal Father. He became man as male, not by accident but because he is Son and not Daughter; because what was to be communicated to the created world in human form in the incarnation was the relation which he has to the Father. . . . And because the ordained priest is not exercising a priesthood of his own but is the agent and instrument through which Christ is exercising *his* priesthood, he too must be male.'[6] Much as I would like I cannot give further space to quotations from Dr Mascall.

It seems to me that Mascall's great mistake is to overlook the fact that the New Testament writings and early Christian practice do not allude to an individualistic official priesthood, but rather refer to the priesthood of all believers, which is a priesthood of the church, of the whole people of God. The New Testament emphasises the access which individual Christians have to the mercy seat of God through Jesus Christ, the Great High Priest (Heb. 10.19–25). It speaks of the people of God collectively as 'a holy priesthood' who are to offer spiritual sacrifices, made acceptable to God through Jesus Christ (1 Pet. 2.5) and as 'a royal priesthood' who are to sing the praises of God who called them out of darkness to his wonderful light (1 Pet. 2.19) and finally as 'a kingdom of priests' loved and cleansed from their sins by Jesus Christ to serve his God and Father (Rev. 1.5, 6; 5.10). It is therefore not so patently obvious or as logical as Mascall would have us believe that the ordained priesthood must be male. Jesus may indeed have taken on male human nature in his incarnation but surely the salvation of humankind is dependent, not on his 'maleness' but rather on his 'humanness', his solidarity with all of us. Moreover, if the purpose of the incarnation was to communicate the relationship between Father and Son, as a relationship between male persons rather than between persons then how can the incarnation communicate to the female species? It is dangerous to draw such literalist conclusions from the relationships which exist within the mysterious trinity of 'persons' which is the Godhead. This surely is to take analogical reasoning beyond its acceptable limits.

To my mind Richard Hanson's understanding of ministerial priesthood within the Christian church, as argued for in *Christian Priesthood Examined*, makes much more sense in terms of New Testament theology, early Christian practice, the manifest human proclivity for priesthood to be seen in the world's religions and Reformation insights.[7] On Hanson's understanding 'priesthood consists of a ministry of men or women who stand for God to their fellow-men and represent their fellow-men to God.' Such priesthood is truly representative – a reflection and expression on earth of Christ's priesthood, and also a channelling or concentration of the priesthood of all Christians, a representation of the church's priesthood. And there is no valid argument, theological, historical or sociological, which should prevent a woman today from exercising such a priesthood if she is called by God and set apart by the church. It is a priesthood which derives its delegated authority from two sources: Jesus Christ the Great High Priest and the priestly calling of his body, the church.

3. Authority

The most prevalent evangelical objection to the ordination of women centres on the issue of authority. As already argued in chapter 3, I believe that Paul's attitude to the question of authority within the church and in the home was dictated by his concern for the spread of the gospel in the world of his time and the maintenance of order in society.[9] For this reason, many of his injunctions are irrelevant today. Moreover, Jesus' own authority was not dependent on his training or position in society – he was neither a recognised rabbi nor married – but was rather derived from his Father in heaven. It was also an 'unworldly' authority, exercised through obedient service, even to death. Similarly, all authority given to the church is derived or delegated and is given to all disciples. Consequently, it may be argued, on a parallel with priesthood, official leadership in the church comes only by the call of God and according to the will of the people. The authority thus given, an authority to serve God and man, cannot be said to belong by right to one sex rather than another any more than it belongs any longer to one particular race.

Conclusions

If, therefore, there exist no valid grounds, theological, historical or sociological, on which to continue to argue for male priesthood and male leadership, and the barring of women from the ordained ministry, it is to be hoped that very soon, throughout the world, women called by God and set apart by the church will begin to exercise their priestly service as ordained ministers of the gospel in Christ's church. Only in a whole church (of equal men and women) with a whole ministry (of women and men equally) will a whole gospel serve the whole need of the whole world.

Notes

CHAPTER 1 (pp. 15–19)

1 'Polygyny' is the precise term by which to refer to a system of marriage
which allows a man to have more than one wife; in general usage it is
often replaced by the inclusive 'polygamy' which refers to having more
than one partner of either sex. 'Bridewealth' refers to the marriage
settlement in cash or kind given by the family of the bridegroom to
the family of the bride, while 'dowry' refers to the assets brought by
the bride.

CHAPTER 2 (pp. 23–36)

1 Up to the fourth century AD all Christians accepted the books of
the Greek-speaking rather than the Hebrew-speaking Jews and these
included the books now known as the Apocrypha. At that time they
were placed by Jerome in an inferior position in the Vulgate. Later,
at the Reformation, all churches belonging to the Reformed Tradition
demoted them while the Council of Trent on behalf of the Roman
Catholic Church declared them fully canonical.
2 Larry Christenson, *The Christian Family* (London: Fountain Trust,
1971).
3 Susan Dowell & Linda Hurcombe, *Dispossessed Daughters of Eve: Faith
and Feminism* (London: SCM Press, 1981).
4 Quoted from 'Gospel and Culture' (The Willowbank Report) in
*Explaining the Gospel in Today's World: Church Planting; Gospel and
Culture*, Lausanne Occasional Papers 1 & 2 (London: SU, 1978) pp.
18–20. The same report continues: 'The controversial question of
the status of women was not debated at our Consultation. But we
acknowledge the need to search for an understanding which attempts
with integrity to do justice to all the biblical teaching, and which sees
the relations between men and women as being both rooted in the
created order and at the same time wonderfully transformed by the
new order which Jesus introduced' (p. 20).

5 Elisabeth S. Fiorenza, 'Feminist Theology and New Testament Interpretation', *JSOT* 22 (1982) pp. 34–5.

6 Cf. any commentary on Genesis or Introduction to the Old Testament for pentateuchal criticism and a discussion of the Genesis sources. The Yahwist source is marked by the use of 'Yahweh' to denote God and the Priestly by 'Elohim'.

7 G. A. F. Knight, *A Christian Theology of the Old Testament* (London: SCM Press, 2nd Ed., 1964) p. 25; cf. Paul K. Jewett, *Man as Male and Female* (Grand Rapids: Eerdmans, 1975) passim.

8 Cf. Derek Kidner, *Genesis: An Introduction and Commentary* (London: Tyndale Press, 1967) ad loc.; Gerhard von Rad, *Genesis: A Commentary* (London: SCM Press, 2nd Ed., 1963) ad loc. See also on the creation accounts: Gerhard von Rad, *Old Testament Theology*, Vol. 1 (Edinburgh: Oliver & Boyd, 1962); Walther Eichrodt, *Theology of the Old Testament*, Vol. 2 (London: SCM Press, 1967); and Hans Walter Wolff, *Anthropology of the Old Testament* (London: SCM Press, 1974).

9 Joyce Baldwin, 'How to Create a Woman', *His Magazine* 33 8 (May 1973) pp. 8–9.

10 Eichrodt, op. cit., p. 24; Jewett, op. cit., passim.

11 Von Rad, *Genesis*, p. 91.

12 Kidner, *Genesis*, p. 71.

13 Ibid., p. 70.

14 Wolff, op. cit., pp. 166–76; Marie de Merode de Croy, 'The Role of Woman in the Old Testament', *Concilium* 134 (1980) pp. 71–9.

15 Cf. Albrecht Oepke, 'γυνή', G. Kittel (ed.) & G. W. Bromiley (trans.) *Theological Dictionary of the New Testament* (Grand Rapids: Eerdmans, 1964) Vol. 1, pp. 776–89, esp. p. 781.

16 Ibid. It is important to note that the 'people' of Israel, addressed for example by Moses on Mt Sinai (Exod. 19.14–15), are 'a religious community composed in the first instance exclusively of males, or perhaps originally of all adult males' (cf. Phyllis Bird, 'Images of Women in the Old Testament' in Rosemary Radford Ruether (ed.) *Religion and Sexism: Images of Woman in the Jewish and Christian Traditions* (New York: Simon & Schuster, 1974) pp. 41–88, esp. pp. 48–57).

CHAPTER 3 (pp. 37–57)

1 Cf. Albrecht Oepke,'γυνή', loc. cit., pp. 776–9.

2 Ibid and various.

3 Oepke, loc. cit., p. 777.

4 Ibid.

5 Cf. E. M. Blaiklock, *From Prison in Rome – Letters to the Philippians*

and Philemon (Grand Rapids: Zondervan, 1964), p. 47. He writes: 'Macedonian inscriptions bear witness to the respected and responsible position of women in the northern Greek communities.'

6 Quoted in Simone de Beauvoir, *The Second Sex* (Harmondsworth: Penguin, 1972) p. 119.

7 Letha Scanzoni & Nancy Hardesty, *All We're Meant to Be: A Biblical Approach to Women's Liberation* (Waco, Texas: Word Books, 1974) pp. 50–51.

8 Quoted in Thomas Boslooper. *The Image of Woman* (New York: UTS, 1980) p. 13.

9 Quoted in Scanzoni & Hardesty, op. cit., pp. 76–7.

10 Oepke, loc. cit., pp. 778–9.

11 Ibid, pp. 780–81. Scanzoni & Hardesty, op. cit., pp. 51–2.

12 Quoted with original sources in Joachim Jeremias, *Jerusalem in the Time of Jesus* (London: SCM Press, 1969) p. 360.

13 Oepke, op. cit., pp. 781–4.

14 Jeremias, op. cit., pp. 372–5.

15 Increasingly commentators are moving away from the medieval interpretation of Mary as an example of the contemplative life and Martha of the active, and recognising the incident for what it is: a vindication of the rights of woman to be a student of the law. Cf. for example E. E. Ellis, *The Gospel of Luke* (London: Nelson, 1966) ad loc.; Rosemary Radford Ruether, *Mary – The Feminine Face of the Church* (London: SCM Press, 1979) p. 70.

16 Rosemary Radford Ruether, op. cit., pp. 68–9.

17 Alfred Edersheim, *The Life and Times of Jesus the Messiah* (London: Longmans, Green & Co., 1906) pp. 745–7; sources differ.

18 Cf. Jeremias, op. cit., p. 376.

19 See my article 'Spirit-Possession, Exorcism and Social Context: An Anthropological Perspective with Theological Implications', *Churchman* 94, 3 (1980) pp. 226–45 for full documentation of this widely-known phenomenon; also my 'Charismatics and Liturgy' prepared for the BSA Sociology of Religion Study Group Conference at Bristol, March-April 1982, an edited version of which is forthcoming in *Churchman*.

20 See Elisabeth S. Fiorenza, 'Women in the Early Christian Movement' in Carol P. Christ & Judith Plaskow (eds), *Womanspirit Rising* (San Francisco: Harper & Row, 1979) pp. 84–92. The words are *diakonos* and *prostatis* translated when used of man as 'deacon' and 'leader', but as 'deaconess' and 'helper' for woman.

21 Evelyn & Frank Stagg, *Woman in the World of Jesus* (Edinburgh: St Andrew Press, 1978) p. 163.

22 Hans Dieter Betz, *Galatians* (Philadelphia: Fortress Press, 1979), p. 181.

23 Ibid. p. 189. Numerous commentators deny the political and social consequences of this statement, allowing only the religious. Betz discusses the matter quite thoroughly.

24 Ibid for a discussion of the practice and significance of ritual at baptism.

25 John Bligh in his *Galatians* (London: St Paul Publications, 1969) p. 328 quotes approvingly W. Rauschenbusch: 'Paul was a radical in theology, but a social conservative.'

26 For a general discussion of the passage and the androgynous Christ-Anthropos see Betz, *Galatians*, pp. 181–201; also commentaries ad loc.; Paul K. Jewett, *Man as Male and Female*, passim, but especially pp. 142–7; and Elisabeth S. Fiorenza, 'Women in the Early Christian Movement', loc. cit., p. 88.

27 Jean Héring, *The First Epistle of Saint Paul to the Corinthians* (London: Epworth Press, 1962) p. 48.

28 Jewett, op. cit., passim.

29 F. F. Bruce, *1 & 2 Corinthians* (London: Oliphants, 1971) ad loc. Abstinence of from 7 to 30 days is permitted in the Mishnah.

30 Hans Conzelmann, *1 Corinthians* (Philadelphia: Fortress Press, 1975) ad loc.

31 Ibid. The verbs are *aphienai* and *chōristhēnai*. In v. 10 'separate' is used of the wife and in v. 11 'divorce' of the husband but in v. 13 'divorce' is used of the wife.

32 Jewett, op. cit., p. 53 and sources.

33 The rabbinic exegesis (exegesis of Jewish rabbis) here referred to is that which ignored the creation account of Genesis 1 and inferred the inferiority and subordination of woman because of her subsequent creation from Adam's rib as narrated in Genesis 2 and the curse of the fall as recorded in Genesis 3. For reasons of argument and space I am not concerned with the exegetical details of 1 Cor. 11. My thesis requires a fresh hermeneutical approach and the recognition of Gal. 3.28 as the pivotal Pauline text. For further discussion of 1 Cor. 11 see the commentaries ad loc and the following articles and monographs: Robert Banks, 'Paul and Women's Liberation', *Interchange* 18 (1976) pp. 81–105; G. B. Caird, *Paul and Women's Liberty* (Manchester: John Rylands Library, 1972); M. D. Hooker, 'Authority on Her Head: An Examination of 1 Cor. XI. 10', *New Testament Studies* 10 (1964) pp. 410–16; William J. Martin, '1 Corinthians 11:2–26: An Interpretation' in W. W. Gasque & R. P. Martin, *Apostolic History and the Gospel* (Exeter: Paternoster Press, 1970) pp. 231–41. For the 'traditional' conservative evangelical viewpoint, arguing for the subordination of woman to man in the family and in the church, see the recently-published books by James B. Hurley, *Man and Woman in Biblical Perspective* (Leicester: IVP, 1981) and

Stephen B. Clark, *Man and Woman in Christ: An Examination of the Roles of Men and Women in Light of Scripture and the Social Sciences* (Ann Arbor: Servant Books, 1980, distributed in the UK by T & T Clark, Edinburgh).

39 Cf. Martin Dibelius & Hans Conzelmann, *The Pastoral Epistles* (Philadelphia: Fortress Press, 1966) pp. 44–9.

40 In an essay entitled 'Culture and the New Testament' in John R. W. Stott & Robert Coote (eds), *Down to Earth: Studies in Christianity and Culture* (London: Hodder & Stoughton, 1981) pp. 22–3 Howard Marshall criticises Paul Jewett's hermeneutic in his *Man as Male and Female*. I am not sure that Marshall has fully understood Jewett, but even if he has I do not believe my thesis lays itself open to the same criticism.

41 Elisabeth S. Fiorenza, 'Feminist Theology and New Testament Interpretation', loc. cit., pp. 34–5. The passages of Scripture which state that woman is made in the image of God and that this image is restored in Christ are *descriptive* of God's intention for woman; the passages which exhort woman to be subordinate to man are *prescriptive* of man's desire for woman to behave as the social system requires, which happens to be a patriarchal social order.

CHAPTER 4 (pp. 58–83)

1 David Greene & Frank O'Connor (eds & trans), *A Golden Treasury of Irish Poetry 600–1200* (London: Macmillan, 1967) p. 158.

2 Elisabeth Elliot in her *Let Me Be a Woman: Notes on Womanhood for Valerie* (London: Hodder & Stoughton, 1979) gives a similar modern view (p. 24).

3 *Gnosticism*, deriving its name from the Greek *gnosis* meaning 'knowledge', was prevalent in the church in the second century and emphasised in its many sects special knowledge received by secret tradition from the apostles or by direct revelation. *Montanism*, deriving its name from one Montanus, arose in the second century as an apocalyptic movement, emphasising the outpouring of the Spirit on the church, the first manifestations occurring in the lives of Montanist prophets and prophetesses. In third century North Africa the church Father, Tertullian, became a Montanist.

4 On this subject see Jean Daniélou, *The Ministry of Women in the Early Church* (London: The Faith Press, 1961) pp. 9–11.

5 I use the word 'deacon' rather than 'deaconess' to translate the Greek *diakonos* (masculine) as the feminine *diakonissa* does not occur in the literature until the Council of Nicea in AD 325.

6 Polycarp, *ep. ad Philippenses* 4.3; Ignatius, *ep. ad Smyrnaeos* 13.1;

Hermas, *Visions* 2.3. Cf. Daniélou, op. cit., pp. 13–14 and Ida Raming, 'From the Freedom of the Gospel to the Petrified "Men's Church": The Rise and Development of Male Domination in the Church', *Concilium* 134 (1980) pp. 3–13.

7 Clement, *paedagogus* 3.12, 97; Origen, *de oratione* 28.4 and homilies on Luke 17 & Isaiah 6; Tertullian, *de virginibus velandis* 9.2; *ad uxorem* 1, 3, 4; *de monogamia* 11.1, 4; 12.1.

8 Tertullian, *de pudicitia* 13.4.

9 *Egyptian Church Order* quoted in Daniélou, op. cit., p. 18.

10 Tertullian, *de praescriptio* 41.5 (cf. *de baptismo* 17.4); *de virginibus velandis* 9.1.

11 So Raming after Bangerter, op. cit., pp. 8, 13.

12 Origen, *ep. ad Romanos* 10.17.

13 Clement, *stromateis* 3.6.53.

14 Canon 19 of the Council of Nicea seems to bear witness to this and Canon 15 of the Council of Chalcedon (AD 451) is explicit. But it is an Eastern not a Western custom and at the Western Council of Orange (AD 441) we read: 'deaconesses should not be in any way ordained.'

15 Daniélou, op. cit., pp. 20–28. The *Didache* and the *Didascalia Apostolorum* are important sources.

16 Raming, loc. cit., p. 9; on this section as a whole see Janet Grierson, *The Deaconess* (London: CIO Publishing, 1981) pp. 1–15, and here pp. 8–9.

17 Bernard P. Prusak, 'Woman: Seductive Siren and Source of Sin' in Rosemary Radford Ruether (ed.), *Religion and Sexism*, pp. 89–116.

18 Justin, *apologia* 1.5.2; 2.5.3 ff.; Irenaeus, *adversus haereses*, passim; Clement, *paedagogus* 2.3; *stromateis*; Origen, *contra Celsum*; Tertullian, *adversus Marcionem* 5; *apologeticus* 22; *de patientia* 5; *de virginibus velandis* 7; *de carne Christi* 17.

19 On the uncleanness of children see Origen, *in Leviticum* 8.3; 12.4.

20 Clement, *paedagogus* 3.11.

21 Tertullian, *de cultu feminarum* 1.1.

22 On this section as a whole see Rosemary Radford Ruether, 'Misogynism and Virginal Feminism in the Fathers of the Church' in *Religion and Sexism*, pp. 150–83.

23 Gregory of Nyssa, *de opificio hominis* 16, 17.

24 Augustine, *de sermone Dom. in monte* 2.41.

25 Jerome to Demetrias, *ep.* 130.10.

26 Augustine, *confessiones* 9.

27 Jerome to Asella, *ep.* 45.2–7.

28 In the *Gospel of Thomas* (c AD 140) we read: 'Simon Peter said to them [the disciples]: "Let Mary leave us, for women are not worthy of Life." Jesus said, "I myself shall lead her, in order to make her male,

so that she too may become a living spirit, resembling you males. For every woman who will make herself male will enter the Kingdom of Heaven." ' Cf. Elaine Pagels, *The Gnostic Gospels* (New York: Random House, 1979) p. 47.

29 Radford Ruether, 'Misogynism', loc. cit., p. 179.

30 On this section as a whole see Eleanor Commo McLaughlin, 'Equality of Souls, Inequality of Sexes: Woman in Medieval Theology' in *Religion and Sexism*, pp. 213–66.

31 R. W. Southern, *Western Society and the Church in the Middle Ages* (Harmondsworth: Penguin, 1970) p. 310.

32 Julian of Norwich, *Revelations of Divine Love* 51, 52, 54, 59.

33 Joan Dempsey Douglass, 'Women and the Continental Reformation' in *Religion and Sexism*, pp. 292–318.

34 Martin Luther 'To Three Nuns', *Luther: Letters of Spiritual Counsel* (Library of Christian Classics 18, London: SCM Press, 1955) pp. 270–72.

35 John Calvin in *Calvin: Institutes of the Christian Religion* (Library of Christian Classics 20, London: SCM Press, 1960) pp. 405 ff. (2.8.42 ff.).

36 Roland Bainton, *Women of the Reformation* (3 vols Minneapolis: Augsburg, 1971–77) 1, *In Germany and Italy*, pp. 23–44, 55–76.

37 Robert F. Wearmouth, *Methodism and the Common People of the Eighteenth Century* (London: Epworth Press, 1945) p. 223, quoted by Donald W. Dayton. I am grateful to my friend Donald Dayton for providing me with articles on which I have relied heavily: 'Evangelical Roots of Feminism', *The Covenant Quarterly* 34 4 (November 1976) pp. 41–56; with Lucille Sider Dayton, 'Women as Preachers: Evangelical Precedents', *Christianity Today* 19 17 (May 1975) pp. 4–7 and others containing similar material.

38 Abel Stevens, *The Women of Methodism* (New York: Carlton Porter, 1806) pp. 63–4.

39 Commenting on Gal. 3.8 in *The Holy Bible* in various editions, quoted by Dayton.

40 Jonathan Blanchard & N. L. Rice, *A Debate on Slavery* (Cincinnati: William H. Moore, 1846) p. 433, quoted by Dayton.

41 B. T. Roberts, *Ordaining Women* (Rochester, New York: Earnest Christian Publishing House, 1891) p. 13, quoted by Dayton.

42 The Holiness Movement in America, dating from the mid-nineteenth century, tried to keep alive distinctive Methodist teaching on entire sanctification by faith (as an experience subsequent to conversion) and the Christian perfectionism of John Wesley.

43 The Oxford Movement (1833–45) aimed at restoring the High Church ideals of the seventeenth century in the Church of England.

44 After Ray Strachey, *The Cause: A Short History of the Women's*

Movement in Great Britian (first published in 1928, re-issued London: Virago, 1978) pp. 212–15, quoting army regulations.

45 Janet Grierson, op. cit., pp. 16–25.

46 The 'zenana' was the part of the house in which women of high castes were secluded in India and Iran.

47 J. G. Baldwin, 'Does Jill's Christian Ministry Add Anything to Jack's?', *BEFMS* 9 (1979) pp. 16–25; C. P. Williams, ' "Powerful Arms of the Church of God": Women Missionary Candidates in the Late Nineteenth Century (A Protestant Perspective)', *BEFMS* 9 (1979) pp. 26–45.

CHAPTER 5 (pp. 84–114)

1 Cf. G. B. Caird, *The Gospel of St Luke* (Harmondsworth: Penguin, 1963) ad loc.; E. Earle Ellis, *The Gospel of Luke* (London: Nelson, 1966) ad loc.; I. Howard Marshall, *The Gospel of Luke* (Exeter: Paternoster Press, 1978) ad loc.; Rosemary Radford Ruether, *Mary – The Feminine Face of the Church* (London: SCM Press, 1979) p. 70.

2 Simone de Beauvoir, *The Second Sex*, pp. 128–39, especially p. 135.

3 Ibid., p. 139; cf. Lawrence Stone, *The Family, Sex and Marriage in England 1500–1800* (London: Weidenfeld & Nicolson, 1977) pp. 336–43.

4 De Beauvoir, op. cit., p. 161, where the author comments: 'The women who have accomplished works comparable to those of men are those exalted by the power of social institutions above all sexual differentiation. Queen Isabella, Queen Elizabeth, Catherine the Great were neither male nor female – they were sovereigns. . . . Religion works the same transformation. . . .'

5 Alice S. Rossi, 'Social Roots of the Woman's Movement' in Alice S. Rossi (ed.), *The Feminist Papers: From Adams to de Beauvoir* (New York: Columbia University Press, 1974) pp. 250–52; Barbara Welter, 'The Cult of True Womanhood: 1820–1860', *American Quarterly* 18 (1966) pp. 151–74.

6 John Charvet, *Feminism* (London: Dent, 1982) pp. 1, 146; Janet Radcliffe Richards, *The Sceptical Feminist* (Harmondsworth: Penguin, 1980) pp. 13–14; cf. Elizabeth Elliot, *Let Me Be a Woman*, pp. 125–7 where the feminist view of equality is mis-understood.

7 Mary Astell, *Reflections upon Marriage* (1700, no pagination) quoted in Juliet Mitchell, 'Women and Equality' in Juliet Mitchell & Ann Oakley (eds) *The Rights and Wrongs of Women* (Harmondsworth: Penguin, 1976) pp. 379–99.

8 Mary Astell, quoted in Mitchell, loc. cit., p. 388.

9 Mary Wollstonecraft, *Vindication of the Rights of Woman* (Harmondsworth: Penguin, 1975 [1792]) p. 263.

10 John Stuart Mill, 'The Subjection of Women' in Richard Wollheim (ed.), *John Stuart Mill, Three Essays: On Liberty, Representative Government, The Subjection of Women* (Oxford: OUP, 1975) p. 427.

11 Ibid., p. 481; cf. remainder of paragraph.

12 Cf. Olive Banks, *Faces of Feminism: A Study of Feminism as a Social Movement* (Oxford: Martin Robertson, 1981) p. 26.

13 Phoebe Palmer, *The Promise of the Father* (Boston: Henry V. Degen, 1859) p. 341, quoted in an unpublished article kindly loaned me by Donald W. Dayton, 'Prophesying Daughters: The Ministry of Women in the Holiness Traditions' (1980) p. 12.

14 F. de L. Booth-Tucker, *The Life of Catherine Booth* (3 vols London: The Salvation Army, 1893) Vol. 1, p. 123.

15 Catherine Booth, quoted in Catherine Bramwell-Booth, *Catherine Booth: The Story of Her Loves* (London: Hodder & Stoughton, 1970) pp. 50, 51, 52, 89, 181, 182.

16 John Charvet, op. cit., pp. 48–54.

17 Ibid., pp. 54–61.

18 Ibid., pp. 69–78.

19 Banks, op. cit., p. 100 and passim.

20 Richard J. Evans, *The Feminists: Women's Emancipation Movements in Europe, America and Australasia 1840–1920* (London: Croom Helm, Rev. Ed. 1979) p. 125.

21 Quoted by Charvet, op. cit., pp. 21–2.

22 Ibid., pp. 124–37.

23 Quoted in Evans, op. cit., p. 49.

24 Evans, op. cit., pp. 44–63; Banks, op. cit., pp. 13–27, 28–34, 44–67, 63–84.

25 Evans, op. cit., pp. 63–9; Banks, op. cit., pp. 13–27.

26 Cf. Ray Strachey, *The Cause: A Short History of the Women's Movement in Great Britain* (London: Virago Reprint, 1978) passim for a lively and detailed account.

27 Ibid.

28 Betty Friedan, *The Feminine Mystique* (Harmondsworth: Penguin, 1965 [1963]) passim.

29 Banks, op. cit., pp. 207 ff.

30 Banks, op. cit., pp. 207–63; Charvet, op. cit., pp. 97–135.

31 See *Time* magazine, July 12, 1982, pp. 47–8.

32 Betty Friedan, *The Second Stage* (London: Michael Joseph, 1982 [1981]) pp. 61, 89–129.

CHAPTER 6 (pp. 117-32)

1 See above pp. 27–8.

2 Paul Tournier, *The Gift of Feeling* (London: SCM Press, 1981 [1979]) p. 62; cf. his *The Meaning of Persons* (London: SCM Press, 1957).

3 Eduard Schweizer, *The Good News according to Mark* (London: SPCK, 1971) ad loc.; Raymond Brown, *The Gospel according to John* (2 vols London: Geoffrey Chapman, 1971) Vol. 1, ad loc.; also the major commentators on all four Gospels.

4 Elisabeth Moltmann-Wendel, *The Women around Jesus: Reflections on Authentic Personhood* (London: SCM Press, 1982) p. 101.

5 Ibid., 92–104; Tournier, *The Gift of Feeling*, pp. 90–93.

6 Quoted in Tournier, *The Gift of Feeling*, pp. 97–8.

7 Marabel Morgan, *The Total Woman* (London: Hodder & Stoughton, 1975 [1973]).

8 Ibid., pp. 18–22.

9 Ibid., pp. 55, 76, 80.

10 Ibid., pp. 94–9.

11 Ibid., pp. 186–8.

12 See above p. 101.

13 Betty Friedan, *The Second Stage*, pp. 68–9.

14 Tournier, *The Gift of Feeling*, pp. 64–5.

15 Martin Buber, *I and Thou*, translated and edited by Walter Kaufmann (New York: Charles Scribner's Sons, 1970) passim.

16 Elisabeth Elliot, *The Mark of a Man* (London: Hodder & Stoughton, 1981) pp. 9–13.

17 On this section see the article by Henriette Santer entitled 'Women, Men and Psychology', *Theology* 706 (July 1982) pp. 262–9, brief and to the point; John Archer & Barbara Lloyd, *Sex and Gender* (Harmondsworth: Penguin, 1982); Jean Baker Miller, *Toward a New Psychology of Women* (Harmondsworth: Penguin, 1978 (1976)); Luise Eichenbaum & Susie Orbach, *Outside In . . . Inside Out: Women's Psychology: A Feminist Psychoanalytic Approach* (Harmondsworth: Penguin, 1982); Una Kroll, *Flesh of My Flesh* (London: DLT, 1975).

18 Quoted in Archer & Lloyd, op. cit., p. 9.

19 Cf. Tournier, *The Gift of Feeling*, p. 131 where he quotes Eric Fuchs' *Le désir et la tendresse* (Geneva: Labor et Fides, 1979).

CHAPTER 7 (pp. 133–46)

1 Elisabeth Moltmann-Wendel, *The Women around Jesus*, to which book I am indebted for much in this section.

2 J. N. Sanders & B. A. Mastin, *A Commentary on the Gospel according*

to St John (London: A. & C. Black, 1968) p. 268; cf. other commentators ad loc., especially Raymond Brown, *The Gospel according to John*, Vol. 1; A. Plummer, *The Gospel according to S. John* (Cambridge: CUP, 1896); and C. K. Barrett, *The Gospel according to St John* (1st Ed. London: SPCK, 1955).

3 Moltmann-Wendel, op. cit., p. 20.

4 Guido di Pietro Angelico – called Fra – (1387–1455), great Italian painter and member of the Dominican order.

5 A woman of Jerusalem who, according to a legend (probably of fourteenth century French origin in this form), offered her head-cloth to Jesus to wipe the blood and sweat from his face on the way to Calvary. He returned it with his features impressed upon it.

6 Moltmann-Wendel, op. cit., p. 45.

7 Cf. for this and further definitions Charles Winick, *Dictionary of Anthropology* (New Jersey: Littlefield, Adams & Co., 1970) pp. 202–3.

8 Edward Shorter, *The Making of the Modern Family* (London: Collins/Fontana, 1977 [1975]) passim.

9 Elisabeth Badinter, *The Myth of Motherhood: An Historical View of the Maternal Instinct* (London: Souvenir Press, 1981) passim.

10 Quoted, ibid., p. 62.

11 Shorter, op. cit., p. 15.

12 Ibid.

13 Badinter, op. cit., passim and especially p. 328.

14 The French philosopher, Jean-Jacques Rousseau (1712–78), published his famous treatise on education entitled *Émile* in 1762, advocating the natural goodness and rights of the child and the obligations and duties of parents to facilitate development by providing him with freedom, love and affection.

15 Badinter, op. cit., pp. 327–30.

16 Headed 'Ode on Christmas Day, 1980: On the presentation of a garden fork to my wife' and published in Margaret & Rupert Davies, *Circles of Community* (London: BCC, 1982) p. 4.

17 *Church Times* (London: July 31, 1981) p. 1.

CHAPTER 8 (pp. 147–59)

1 Virginia Woolf, *A Room of One's Own* (London: Granada Publishing, 1977 [1979]) p. 105.

2 Gerhard von Rad, *Genesis*, pp. 57–8; Hans Walter Wolff, *Anthropology of the Old Testament*, pp. 93–8, 159–65.

3 Cf. Joachim Jeremias, *The Parables of Jesus* (Rev. Ed. London: SCM Press, 1963) pp. 58–63; Eduard Schweizer, *The Good News according to Matthew*, ad loc.; Floyd V. Filson, *A Commentary on the Gospel*

according to St Matthew (London: A. & C. Black, 1960) ad loc.; I. Howard Marshall, *The Gospel of Luke*, ad loc.

4 See Catherine Hall, 'History of the Housewife' reprinted from *Spare Rib* 26 (August 1974) in Marsha Rowe (ed.), *Spare Rib Reader* (Harmondsworth: Penguin, 1982) pp. 131–7.

5 Anna Coote & Beatrix Campbell, *Sweet Freedom: The Struggle for Women's Liberation* (London: Pan/Picador, 1982) pp. 48–50.

6 Lesley Garner, *How to Survive as a Working Mother* (Harmondsworth: Penguin, 1982 [1980]) pp. 17–26.

7 For these and other facts see Coote & Campbell, op. cit., pp. 48–50.

8 Quoted, ibid., p. 59.

9 Ibid., p. 183.

10 See Tournier, *The Gift of Feeling*, ch. 6, entitled 'Women at Home and at Work', pp. 42–50.

11 See Jean Baker Miller, *Toward a New Psychology of Women*, pp. 3–13 and passim.

12 On this section as a whole see Janet Radcliffe Richards, *The Sceptical Feminist*, pp. 195–221.

13 Betty Friedan, *The Feminine Mystique*, pp. 32–3 and passim.

14 Margaret Mead, *Male and Female* (Harmondsworth: Penguin, 1962 [1950]) pp. 157–8 and passim.

CHAPTER 9 (pp. 160–71)

1 Billerbeck on Matt. 19.12 quoted in Eduard Schweizer, *The Good News according to Matthew*, ad loc.

2 See Myrtle S. Langley, *The Nandi of Kenya: Life Crisis Rituals in a Period of Change* (London: Hurst, 1979) p. 1.

3 Eduard Schweizer, loc. cit.

4 See, for example: 'Singleness is the Will of God', two memoranda from John H. Yoder to Mennonite Educators, reproduced by permission and kindly passed on to me by Joan M. Miller; David Gillett, Anne Long & Ruth Fowke, *A Place in the Family: The Single Person in the Local Church* (Bramcote, Notts: Grove Books, 1981).

5 It is important to note that contrary to some expositors' teaching on the subject Paul does not view marriage as a *charism* in 1 Cor. 7.7 (cf. Hans Conzelmann, *1 Corinthians*, ad loc.).

6 Jack Dominian, *The Growth of Love and Sex* (London: DLT/NCH, 1982), especially pp. 1–3, 81–91.

7 See Daniel Goergen, *The Sexual Celibate* (New York: Seabury, 1974; London: SPCK, 1976).

8 See Margaret Britton, *The Single Woman in the Family of God* (London: SCM Press, 1982) pp. 79–84.

9 Charles W. Shedd, in *The Stork is Dead* (Waco, Texas and London: Word Books, 1968), teaches young people (including his own children) that masturbation is a gift of God, 'the wise provision of a very wise Creator' (p. 73). Cf. Letha Scanzoni & Nancy Hardesty, *All We're Meant to Be*, pp. 145–68 and Margaret Evening, *Who Walk Alone* (London: Hodder & Stoughton, 1974) pp. 30–37 where the subject is discussed from the standpoint of single adults.

10 Paul Tournier, *A Place for You* (London: SCM Press, 1968).

11 I have deliberately not addressed myself to the subject of homosexuality, due to lack of space. I refer the reader to James B. Nelson, *Embodiment: An Approach to Sexuality and Christian Theology* (London: SPCK, 1979) pp. 152–210 and Peter Coleman, *Christian Attitudes to Homosexuality* (London: SPCK, 1980) passim.

12 For considerations of the single life, in addition to the books already quoted, see Margaret Clarkson, *Single* (Eastbourne; Kingsway Publications, 1980); Janice Glover, *Sense and Sensibility for Single Women* (New York: Doubleday, 1963); Nancy L. Peterson, *The Ever Single Woman: Life Without Marriage* (New York: Quill, 1982); Elspeth Stephenson, *Enjoying Being Single* (Tring: Lion, 1981); and Gini Andrews, *Your Half of the Apple: God and the Single Girl* (Bromley, Kent: STL Books, 1978 [1972]) which is more about 'making the best of' not being married and, perhaps 'still hoping'.

CHAPTER 10 (pp. 172–8)

1 George Macdonald, 'The Sweeper of the Floor' in Hugh Martin (ed.) *A Treasury of Christian Verse* (London: SCM Press, 1959) p. 96.

2 'Probing a "Woman's Place" in Church', *Church Times* (London: November 5, 1982) p. 3.

3 On these verbs see Hermann W. Beyer, 'διακονέω . . .', Karl Heinrich Rengstorf, 'δοῦλος . . .', Hermann Strathmann, 'λατρεύω . . .' in Kittel (ed.) & Bromiley (trans.) op. cit., Vol. 2, pp. 81–93, 261–80; Vol. 4, pp. 58–65.

4 Ronald A. Ward, *Hidden Meaning in the New Testament: New Light from the Old Greek* (London: MM & S, 1969) pp. 72–3.

5 Peter Moore (ed.) *Man, Woman, and Priesthood* (London: SPCK, 1978).

6 Ibid., pp. 22–3.

7 Richard Hanson, *Christian Priesthood Examined* (London: Lutterworth Press, 1979).

8 Ibid., pp. 100–101.

9 See pp. 46–56 above.

JOHN RYLANDS
UNIVERSITY
LIBRARY

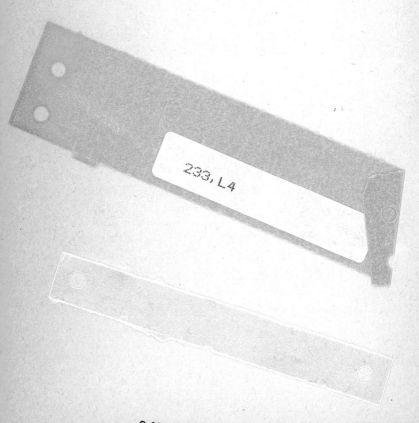

233, L4

-9. SEP. 1985